Foundations
of
Sephardic
Spirituality

T0165661

Foundations
of
Sephardic
Spirituality

The Inner Life of Jews of
the Ottoman Empire

Rabbi Marc D. Angel, PhD

JEWISH LIGHTS Publishing

Foundations of Sephardic Spirituality:
The Inner Life of Jews of the Ottoman Empire

2009 Quality Paperback Edition
© 2006 by Marc D. Angel

Library of Congress Cataloging-in-Publication Data

Angel, Marc.
Foundations of Sephardic spirituality : the inner life of Jews of the Ottoman Empire / Marc D. Angel.
p. cm.
Includes bibliographical references and index.

1. Jews—Turkey—History. 2. Judaism—Turkey—History. 3. Sephardim—History. 4. Sephardim—Religious life. 5. Songs, Ladino. 6. Ladino literature. 7. Turkey—Ethnic relations. I. Title.
DS135.T8A53 2006
296.0956—dc22   2005036840

ISBN: 978-1-58023-341-5 (pbk.)
ISBN: 978-1-68336-067-4 (hc)

Cover design: Tim Holtz
Cover art: "Turkish Chief Rabbi in the Ottoman Empire" © Anita Kushner (www.westbeth.org). Original watercolor on paper, 21" x 28", from *A Magnificence of Dress.*

Manufactured in the United States of America

Published by Jewish Lights Publishing
www.jewishlights.com

This book is dedicated to my beloved uncle
Professor David Romey
Quintessential Sephardic gentleman and scholar

The Ottoman Empire, 1481–1683

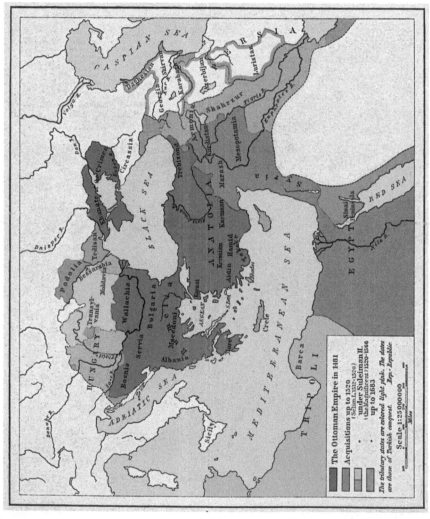

Contents

Acknowledgments

I thank the Board of Trustees of Congregation Shearith Israel in New York City for having granted me a sabbatical for the year 2005, thereby enabling me to devote my full attention to researching and writing this book. A special thanks must go to my son, Rabbi Hayyim Angel, who assumed the full rabbinic responsibilities at Shearith Israel during my sabbatical year. I have been blessed to be associated with Shearith Israel since 1969, and I am grateful to our congregational family for their thoughtfulness and kindness over the years.

I express sincere gratitude to Stuart M. Matlins, publisher of Jewish Lights, and his entire staff for their professional talents—and for really believing in the importance of this book. Stuart Matlins has the unique combination of practical know-how and a searching, idealistic mind. His commitment to this book has meant very much to me. A special word of gratitude goes to the editorial and production staff, including Emily Wichland, Bryna Fischer, and Lauren Seidman. I thank Randall and Hannah Miryam Belinfante for their research assistance.

I had the privilege of growing up in a wonderful extended family, steeped in the traditions of Judeo-Spanish civilization. My debt to my parents—Victor B. and Rachel Romey Angel, of blessed memory—is profound beyond what words can express. This book owes much to them, to my grandparents, uncles and aunts, elder relatives and friends who maintained a mini-Judeo-Spanish civilization in

Seattle. My mother's brother, my Uncle Dave Romey, was an especially strong influence on me and so many others. Uncle Dave was for many years a professor of Spanish, most recently at Portland State University. His academic knowledge was accompanied by a deep traditionalism, pride in Sephardic culture, and congenial personality. In his own quiet way, he has served as an exemplar of Sephardic civilization.

My wife Gilda, the light of my life, has been an infinite source of strength and inspiration to me. I thank her and our children—Rabbi Hayyim Angel, Dr. Dan and Ronda Angel Arking, and Dr. James and Elana Angel Nussbaum—for their love and devotion. A Ladino proverb has it that *hijos de mis hijos, dos vezes mis hijos,* "the children of my children are two times my children." I can fully appreciate the meaning of this proverb as it relates to our beloved grandchildren: Jake Nussbaum, Andrew Arking, Jonathan Marc Arking, and Max Nussbaum.

I close with a blessing to the Almighty, who has given me life, sustained me, and brought me to this special moment.

1

The Inner Life of the Sephardim

I was born and raised in the Sephardic community of Seattle, Washington. I grew up among elders who had come to America from Turkey and the Island of Rhodes, and who spoke a form of medieval Spanish variously known as Judeo-Spanish, Ladino, Spanyol, and Judezmo. Growing up in Seattle with Turkish-born grandparents who spoke an old Spanish language seemed quite natural and normal to me!

My maternal grandfather, Marco Romey (1890–1963), was born in Tekirdag, a Turkish port town on the Sea of Marmara. He was part of a long-standing Sephardic Jewish community in the Ottoman Empire that dated itself back to the arrival of Sephardic exiles from Spain in 1492. In 1908, he was among those Turkish Sephardim who migrated to America.

He arrived in Seattle with little formal education, no knowledge of English, very little money. He found work as a longshoreman, and later became a barber. He never attained anything approaching financial affluence.

In 1911, my maternal grandmother, Sultana Policar (1893–1960), left her hometown on the Island of Marmara in Turkey at the age of eighteen, also to find her future in America. She first went to Portland, Oregon, where she lived with an older sister, Calo.

On a visit to Seattle, she and my grandfather met and soon decided to marry, which they did on May 23, 1912. Like my grandfather, my grandmother had been raised in a Turkish Sephardic community with a long historical memory in the Ottoman Empire. She, too, had received little formal education and grew up in relative poverty.

My grandparents' mother tongue was Judeo-Spanish, a language rooted in medieval Spain and transplanted into the lands of the Ottoman Empire. Although their families had been living in Turkey for over four hundred years, they could not speak Turkish except for a few stray words, often mispronounced with a Spanish accent. They and all their relatives and friends conversed exclusively in Judeo-Spanish; they sang Judeo-Spanish ballads and love songs; they peppered their conversations with Judeo-Spanish proverbs and expressions. Their seven children, including my mother, learned Judeo-Spanish as their mother tongue and did not learn English until they attended public school.

My paternal grandparents, Bohor Yehudah (1867–1925) and Bulissa Huniu Angel (1870–1939), came to Seattle from the Island of Rhodes. They, too, were part of a vibrant Judeo-Spanish-speaking community. My grandfather Angel left Rhodes in 1908 to join his oldest son, Moshe, who had already settled in Seattle. Together, they earned enough money to bring my grandmother Angel and her other six children to America—in 1911. My father, born in 1913, was the only American-born child in his family. My grandfather Angel worked as part-time sexton and Hebrew teacher in the synagogue of Rhodes Jews in Seattle, Congregation Ezra Bessaroth. He also worked in a shoeshine stand, owned together with his son Moshe. My grandmother Angel was known for her skill at home remedies and magical cures, folk traditions she had brought with her from Rhodes. Like my grandparents Romey, my grandparents Angel were good people with little formal education, little money, and few visible signs of material success.

Viewed from the outside, my grandparents and their generation of Sephardim would have appeared to be like other poor immigrants struggling to make a new life in America. They were on the lower rungs of the economic, educational, and cultural ladders. They lacked fluency in English, certainly in their early years here, and had few friends outside their own community. The larger Jewish community in Seattle, composed of Ashkenazic Jews, did not understand the language of the Sephardim—and the Sephardim did not understand Yiddish! So even among their own coreligionists, the Sephardim formed a separate enclave and were often ignored or misunderstood.

In spite of their material and cultural difficulties, the Sephardim saw themselves in a distinctly positive light. My grandfather Romey believed that our family descended from the aristocracy of Jerusalem that had been exiled to Spain in antiquity. We were of the tribe of Judah, the nobility of the Jewish people. We were aristocracy—even if we were temporarily in reduced circumstances! More than merely believing in this widespread Sephardic myth, my grandfather carried himself as though he were indeed a nobleman. He, and so many Sephardim of his generation, walked tall and strong; had remarkable grace and social charm; had inner calm and poise, self-confidence, and pride. The elder Sephardic men and women among whom I was raised did indeed see themselves as "chosen people." This was evident among Sephardim as a whole, not just the Seattle group.

Dr. Louis Hacker, a social worker and a perceptive observer of Sephardic life in New York City, wrote a report in 1926 in which he noted that "the Sephardim consider themselves a people apart. They are 'Spanish Jews,' with a distinct historical consciousness and a pride and dignity that strengthens their unlikeness."[1]

Dr. Cyrus Adler, in an address to the Sisterhood of the Spanish and Portuguese Synagogue of New York City on November 27, 1916, reported that he had visited many Sephardic communities in the Mediterranean lands and had "become reasonably well acquainted with the Sephardic and Oriental Jews in their own home." Dr. Adler found the Sephardim to be "hospitable and generous, simple and proud, their chief characteristic being their independence. The Oriental Jews unless they be decrepit, blind or maimed ask and take no charity and to maintain themselves no work is too hard."[2]

Dr. David de Sola Pool captured the Sephardic spirit in the following words:

> The tradition of a noble past and the possession of an honored family name have never allowed poverty and oppression to degrade the Levantine Jews and rob them of their self-respect. We would be wrong were we to regard an Aboulafia, an Aboab, a Kamhi etc., as members of the lower classes, even though they may be peddlers or shoe polishers. They do not so regard themselves.[3]

A Judeo-Spanish proverb states: *Basta mi nombre ke es Abravanel,* "My name suffices, it is Abravanel." Having an illustrious name like Abravanel was enough to give a person a deep sense of pride and self-respect, a feeling of being part of nobility.

The Ottoman Jewish Milieu of the Nineteenth Century

My grandparents' generation was shaped by the vagaries of history of Jews in the Ottoman Empire. By the time they were born in the late nineteenth century, Ottoman Jewry had undergone several centuries of economic, political, and cultural decline. While there were certainly bright spots in Ottoman Jewish history, the overall picture during the eighteenth and nineteenth centuries included much darkness.

In 1835, an American offered his description of the condition of Istanbul's Jews:

> I think it will hardly be denied that the Jewish nation in Turkey is in a complete state of indigence, as is sufficiently proved by the mean and vile employments to which individuals devote themselves.... There is no appearance of com-

fort, no appearance of competency among them; everything, where sight and smell are concerned, among them is
extremely disgusting, and passing through their quarters,
the sounds that assail the ears prove that they are a querulous race, destitute of domestic peace and comfort.[4]

Yet, this same observer noted with surprise that the Jews maintained "a well regulated republic in the midst of arbitrary power
and anarchy." In spite of his obviously negative view of the condition of Turkish Jews, he admitted that the Jews managed their own
affairs quite well, even though they were living in a difficult political setting.

In 1839, an Armenian resident of Istanbul offered his opinion
of Ottoman Jewry:

The Jews of Turkey, of whom there are about 170,000, are
by no means exempt from the sorrows and curses of their
race. As if conscious that there is no escape from the contempt of the rest of the world, they are willing to undertake
the meanest of earth's callings, literally to "eat the dirt" of
their Muslim masters.... They live in such places as no one
else would inhabit. Their houses are like bee-hives, literally
swarming with human life; even one single room serves for
the only home of several families—and the streets of their
quarters are almost impassable, from the collection of
garbage and all sorts of refuse which are indiscriminately
thrown from the windows of their dwellings.

He concedes that there were a few families of wealth to be
found among the Jews. While focusing on his very negative views
of Jewish life, though, he adds a comment that was more important
than he realized:

Yet it is most amusing to see them on a Jewish Sabbath. The
filthy gabardines which they wore in the week, as they

exercised their various callings, being laid aside, and bright and gaudy finery substituted, in which they strut about the streets, seeming to be other beings, and to have no relation to the wretches of yesterday.[5]

He was surprised to see the Jews on their Sabbath day dressing and behaving as though they were not oppressed, destitute people. Rather, the Jews saw themselves as free and honorable individuals, serving their God by donning their finest clothes and eating their finest meals. While "seeming to be other beings" on the Sabbath, they were in fact the same people; but they were infused with the inner strength and respect with which their religious faith endowed them. Outside observers did not appreciate the inner life of the Jews, often contenting themselves with derogatory evaluations of Jewish poverty and powerlessness.

Outside and Inside Views

A dissonance existed between the external conditions of the Sephardim and their internal perceptions of their lives. This was true not only in their feelings of nobility and independence, but also in the optimistic and life-affirming views they held in spite of their poor economic situation.

In 1908, an observer of the ancient Jewish community in the Balat neighborhood of Istanbul described the "sad hovels of the Jews."[6] In 1918, another visitor to the old Jewish neighborhoods on the Golden Horn wrote that

> these villages are undeniably the most pitiful suburbs that can be seen in Constantinople, where the lower classes live in makeshift shelters. One only sees there hovels, all lopsided in stinking alleyways with greenish puddles.

He noted that "the Turkish Jew never ceased being oppressed."[7]

Mr. A. H. Navon, who had been a director of a school of the Alliance Israélite Universelle, wrote a novel in which he described the neighborhood of Balat as a place

> with leprous hovels, alleys covered in winter as in summer with mud legendary even in the Jewish quarters of the Orient. In spite of the nearby sea, the air is poisoned by an unidentifiable stench of frying, rotten eggs and herring.[8]

If these outside observers described Balat in such unpleasant terms, how did the Jewish residents of this neighborhood view their own condition? We must be grateful to Professor Marie-Christine Bornes-Varol for her important fieldwork among individuals who had actually had direct experience with Jewish life in Balat.[9] During the years 1980–85, she interviewed seventy-nine people. Forty Jewish informants, originating in Balat and familiar with life in this quarter, were interviewed in their own Judeo-Spanish language. Twenty of them were born before 1921, sixteen were born between 1921 and 1940, and four were born after 1940. The other informants also had direct knowledge of life in Balat. By the time these interviews took place in the 1980s, Balat was no longer home to very many Jews, and the old Jewish neighborhood as it had been earlier in the century no longer existed.

Professor Bornes-Varol writes:

> The first and most striking impression gleaned from these conversations ... was that of a sense of loss of a closely knit community and a unique way of life.... The informants spoke with an air of nostalgia about a quarter that had been huddled around its synagogues, where life flowed according to the rhythms of Jewish festivals and religious beliefs, whatever might be the degree of fortune of its inhabitants.[10]

Informants pointed out that Balat was home not only to poor people; a number of prosperous and influential people lived there as well. The Babani family, manufacturers of uniforms for the government, lived in 1862 in a magnificent, multistoried residence. Around 1913, Isak Babani, an exporter of rugs and brocades, built an impressive home in Balat for his family. Other wealthy families in the neighborhood included the Paltis and Bensions. Balat was the seat of the Jewish religious court of Istanbul and was home to Chief Rabbi Abraham Levi (1835–36) and Chief Rabbi Haim Nahum (1908–20), among other dignitaries.

While some informants corroborated the overcrowded conditions in Balat, many others described the neighborhood in more positive terms, that is, a simple life lacking in comforts but far from the state of abject misery. In Ichtipol, a section of Balat, the typical residence was a wooden one-family home with a small garden leading up to it. The informants stressed the pleasantness of the gardens, where they put up the *sukkah* during the festival of Sukkot. The gardens generally each had a well to provide water for domestic needs. The homes were kept clean. Hygiene standards were in keeping with the general standards of the time, with everyone taking a bath once a week and with the women going regularly to the Turkish baths—that also included a *mikvah* (ritual bath).

The neighborhood had some stone houses owned by the well-to-do. These homes were nicely furnished and quite comfortable. Professor Bornes-Varol suggests that foreign visitors to Balat actually passed along the Golden Horn outside the city walls. They thus would only have seen the outer neighborhood of Balat, known as Karabas. This was indeed a wretched area, but it was only a small part of the Balat quarter. The actual section of Balat was in fact much more diverse, cleaner, and happier than these observers had realized.

All of the informants emphasized the "uniformity of life-styles in the quarter"; that is, social differences based on economic status were mitigated. People showed a deep concern for maintaining the community's unity and cohesiveness, so that there was little tension between rich and poor.

Professor Bornes-Varol learned that

> the Jewish population of Balat held in great esteem its fire-
> men, its boatmen, and its coffeehouse owners. These were
> the people who in time of need rushed to defend the honor
> of the community against various troublemakers. Here again
> the recollections of the inhabitants overshade the common
> image of Balat as a downtrodden, faint-hearted community.[11]

She also found that her informants were nostalgic about how
the Jews of Balat enjoyed speaking Judeo-Spanish openly and
loudly, without being afraid of being overheard by non-Jews. Jewish
fruit and vegetable street vendors called out to customers using
Judeo-Spanish phrases and quips.

Professor Bornes-Varol sums up the results of her study:

> The general picture that emerged from the accounts of our
> informants was quite different [from that given by outside
> observers], even when one allows for a measure of idealiza-
> tion. The majority of the population of Balat was certainly
> poor, although their condition was not as bleak as was gener-
> ally believed. Furthermore, amidst the poverty there were sub-
> stantial islands of comfort and even wealth. But perhaps the
> most important difference pertains to the people's self-image.
> Outsiders saw them as a humble, down-trodden community,
> resigned to their fate, living without hope. The memories of
> the people of Balat, on the other hand, stress the pride of the
> community in its own heritage and culture; the joy of living
> according to its own ways and traditions; the sense of solidar-
> ity and unity; and a feeling of autonomy and self-sufficiency.[12]

Whereas outsiders saw the Jews of Balat as a downtrodden and
discouraged group living in dire poverty, the Jews who actually lived
in Balat had a strikingly different evaluation of their lives. In spite of
prevailing poverty, the people were essentially happy and optimistic;

their lives had the context of age-old religious and social traditions; they felt that they belonged to a large and caring community.

The Example of Rhodes

In 1974, I was completing my doctoral dissertation on the history of the Jews of the Island of Rhodes. In reading through the files on Rhodes at the Alliance Israélite Universelle office in Paris, I came across various documents that shed light on the condition of Jews there during the early twentieth century. The leaders of the Jewish community of Rhodes sent a report, dated February 21, 1900, describing the conditions in their community to the Alliance office in Paris. This was at a time when the Alliance was contemplating establishing a new school in Rhodes. The report was stamped with the seal of Chief Rabbi Moshe Franco, and signed by two lay leaders.

The report indicated that among the Jews of Rhodes were thirteen businessmen, only two or three of whom could be described as relatively prosperous. Thirty heads-of-household were of "modest situation," earning their livelihoods as small merchants and grocers. Seventy-seven Jews engaged in manual labor, including forty shoemakers, five cabinetmakers, four tailors, six tin men, seven bakers, eight butchers, four winemakers, one factory worker, one goldsmith and one gardener. Twenty Jews were employees in various businesses, earning relatively low wages. Of the 280 men who lived in poor conditions, 180 were street porters, 50 were boatmen, and 50 were domestic laborers. This description, written by the leaders of the community, obviously paints a dismal picture of economic life among the Jews of Rhodes at the beginning of the twentieth century.[13]

Writing several years later, Leon Semach—the first director of the Alliance Israélite Universelle school for boys in Rhodes—reported that poverty was widespread among the town's Jewish community. He stated that nearly all of the Jews were living in miserable conditions. Some boys attended school without shoes, dressed in rags. A large number of students required full tuition scholarships; many were so poor that their daily lunch consisted of one piece of dry bread.[14]

In the summer of 1974, my wife, children, and I were visiting my parents and family in Seattle. I was invited to give a lecture on the history of the Jews of Rhodes at Congregation Ezra Bessaroth, the congregation in which I grew up. This congregation was established by Jews from Rhodes—like my paternal grandparents—who had come to Seattle in the first several decades of the twentieth century. A large audience, including quite a few men and women who had grown up in Rhodes, gathered to hear my lecture. When I described the information I had found in the archives of the Alliance Israélite Universelle, many in the audience became visibly upset. A number of them challenged my data. They spoke emotionally and emphatically about how wonderful life had been in Rhodes, how they had enjoyed a strong sense of communal solidarity, how the streets had been filled with Jewish songs and religious observances. I responded by reminding them that I was quoting reliable sources by leaders in the community in Rhodes who were describing what they saw with their own eyes. Jews were very poor. Children came to school without shoes, dressed in rags. Economic conditions were desperate. Indeed, if life had been so good in Rhodes, why did so many Jews leave to come to America? Would any of the people in Seattle want to move back to Rhodes and live in their former homes in the narrow alleyways of the old city?

My critics were not silenced by my response. They said: Yes, we were very poor; yes, many of us had to leave for America and other destinations in order to advance ourselves economically. Nevertheless, in spite of the poverty in Rhodes, life had been very good and very full. They had been happy there and still maintain wonderful memories of the vibrant and loving community in which they had been raised.

Certainly, my critics were idealizing their past; they were remembering—even imagining—all sorts of good qualities to life in Rhodes in the early twentieth century. They were forgetting the very real and serious negative features of their hometown community.

Nevertheless, they were reflecting an important truth. The inner life of a community cannot be measured solely on the basis of material assets. Even when economic conditions were dreadful, people still could have a rich inner life, a powerful feeling of self-worth; they could feel that their lives had meaning; they could be happy.

Light in Their Dwellings

Scholars have done significant research on the history and culture of Sephardim in medieval Spain. Some have written important studies on the Jews of the Ottoman Empire. Monographs exist on various communities, personages, Sephardic folklore, and other topics relating to the Judeo-Spanish historical experience.

A general tendency of scholarship has been to record the precipitous economic, political, and cultural decline of Ottoman Jewry during the eighteenth and nineteenth centuries and to study the attempts at modernization during the latter nineteenth and early twentieth centuries. These are valuable studies that greatly help us to understand the history of the Judeo-Spanish-speaking Jews.

Little has been written, though, on the inner life of these Jews. What spiritual and cultural influences helped them maintain their pride, honor, and sense of well-being—even during the long years when they were in financial and political distress? What were the Jewish, Sephardic, and Ottoman components in their cultural makeup? How are we to understand the phenomenon of Jews living in Turkey and the Balkan countries, who did not speak the language of their land but maintained their own distinctive Hispanic language? How is it that these Jews, many living in poverty, sang medieval Spanish love songs and ballads about kings and queens? How did their customs and social patterns reflect a meaningful philosophy of life? What can we learn from the writings of their sages and from the folk wisdom of their average men and women?

The Sephardic experience in the eighteenth- and nineteenth-century Ottoman Empire demonstrates the triumph of the human spirit in the face of ubiquitous discrimination, poverty, and political weakness. How did the Judeo-Spanish-speaking Jews manage to achieve this spiritual triumph?

To answer these questions, we need to have a firm understanding of their historical experience as well as a sensitive understanding of their ideas, values, and attitudes. We need to be aware of the dark, unpleasant elements in their environments; but we also need to see the spiritual, cultural light in their dwellings that imbued their lives with meaning and honor.

Nostalgic History

As a young graduate student in the early 1920s, Mair Jose Benardete—a Turkish-born Sephardic Jew living in New York—collected Judeo-Spanish *romances* (love songs and ballads) sung by Sephardim in the New York area. A student of Spanish literature, Benardete gathered texts from individuals born in Istanbul, Salonika, Izmir, Rhodes, and other locales and was planning to write a book analyzing these songs from a literary and folkloristic point of view. How and why were these Spanish songs maintained by the Sephardim for over four centuries while they were living in lands where Spanish was not the national language? What role did these songs play in the lives of the Sephardim?

In pondering these and similar questions, Benardete concluded that one could not write comprehensively about the *romances* unless one first understood the civilization in which these songs were sung. He therefore turned to researching and writing a book, which he titled *The Hispanic Culture and Character of the Sephardic Jews*. It was published in New York in 1952 by the Hispanic Institute.[15] He referred to his work as a "nostalgic book." In one sense, it was a historical study like other historical studies. Yet, in another sense it was "nostalgic." It related to a civilization of which he was not merely an academic spectator, but of which he was an organic part. In writing his book, he was both recording history— and reflecting history as a participant. He was a Turkish-born Jew, a native speaker of Judeo-Spanish, and he was attempting to give the historical context of the tradition of which he was part.

In a similar vein, the book I am writing is also "nostalgic." It is an attempt to understand the civilization of the Judeo-Spanish-speaking Jews, by someone who himself was born into this civilization just as it had reached the end of its journey through history.

By the time I was born in 1945, the Americanization process had been well underway among Seattle's Sephardim. While my grandparents' generation continued to speak Judeo-Spanish almost exclusively, my parents' generation spoke Judeo-Spanish to their elders and English to their children. In my generation, most of us spoke only English, although we learned enough Judeo-Spanish to follow the conversations of our elders. Our generation picked up some of the songs and proverbs of the "old world" and certainly some of the mannerisms and attitudes of our forebears. Essentially, though, we were the last generation in history to have experienced Judeo-Spanish civilization as a living (albeit dying) organism. The next generations have not grown up in a society whose members spoke Judeo-Spanish as their mother tongue. We have reached the closing chapter in the history of Judeo-Spanish civilization, and the members of my generation are its last eyewitnesses.

The Judeo-Spanish civilization that flourished in Turkey and the Balkan countries for over four hundred years—and continued to manifest itself in the United States, modern Israel, and else-where for another several generations—is very little known and understood. While this book will present the historical framework of what happened to Sephardic Jewry in the Ottoman Empire, its main concern is with who the Sephardim themselves were and what ideas and attitudes animated their civilization.

It is an attempt, by someone who is himself a product of this civilization, to explore its inner dynamic and meaning.

Intellectual Wisdom and Folk Wisdom

In exploring the Judeo-Spanish civilization that flourished over the past five centuries, we need to examine the various elements that helped shape it. Throughout the centuries, the community was blessed with an elite group of intellectuals who produced important writings both in Hebrew and Ladino. They wrote impressive works of Jewish law, Kabbalah, biblical and Talmudic commentary, midrash, religious devotion, and moral guidance. This "intellectual wisdom" permeated the worldview of the Sephardim of the Ottoman Empire. In addition, the Judeo-Spanish communities were endowed with considerable "folk wisdom," as reflected in their proverbs, stories, and songs, as well as in their customs and social patterns. The intellectual wisdom and folk wisdom were interrelated and together helped to shape—and reflect—the inner world of the Judeo-Spanish-speaking Jews.

The interplay of intellectual and folk wisdom was evident in the worldviews of my grandparents. By the time they came to the United States in the early twentieth century, Judeo-Spanish civilization was already approaching its sunset. Yet, they still embodied the ideas and attitudes—the intellectual and folk wisdom—that had shaped the worldview of their parents and grandparents, going back many generations.

My grandfather Marco Romey was a prime example of the traditionalists of his culture—in his language, attitudes, religious views, mannerisms, and so on. The relatively few books in his home library—typical of the collections in so many other Sephardic homes—provided a glimpse into his soul and that of his peers, and provided important insight into Judeo-Spanish civilization at its twilight.

Being poor, he could afford to buy only a small number of books. The only language he read and understood comfortably was Ladino. He could read Hebrew fluently, but without much comprehension. His library reflected these realities. He owned prayer books and Haggadot, most of which included Ladino translations. He also owned the Bible in Hebrew with Ladino translation. His library included several pamphlets, in Hebrew and Ladino, relating to religious ritual: the penitential prayers (*selihot*)* for the period before Rosh Hashanah; the Book of Ruth; hymns in Ladino sung on Rosh Hashanah. A Book of Psalms was also part of the collection.

The above-mentioned publications reflect the centrality of Jewish religion and the rhythms of the Jewish calendar. They also reflect how the Hebraic sources of Judaism were translated into the vernacular of the Sephardim and how a number of liturgical pieces were recited in Ladino. Indeed, the printed Ladino translations were composed in a more formal and archaic style than spoken Judeo-Spanish, so that the Ladino of liturgical pieces took on a quasi-sacred character of its own.

Sephardic homes like my grandfather's often had volumes of the Mishnah, harking back to the Talmudic tradition. These books were especially studied to commemorate the anniversary of the death of loved ones.

Although my grandfather did not own any of the books of *Me'am Lo'ez,* the classic Ladino biblical encyclopedia whose first volume appeared in Istanbul in 1730, he would borrow a copy from fellow Sephardim who were fortunate enough to own these prized books. Printed in Rashi script (as was virtually all Ladino literature until the twentieth century), he frequently would read from its pages to his family. The *Me'am Lo'ez* was a storehouse of information on the Bible, rabbinic literature, and Jewish law and custom. It also offered moral guidance and advice on dealing with life's problems.

Aside from the religiously oriented books, my grandfather's library included several volumes of *La Historia Judia Universal,* by Haim Isaac Shaki, published in eleven volumes in Istanbul from 1899 to 1928. Shaki was influenced by the growing interest in

---

*A note about transliterations: This book follows the standard Sephardic transliteration of Hebrew, using "kh" for the letter *khaf* and "h" for the letter *het.*

Jewish historical studies in Europe and felt that the Sephardim of Judeo-Spanish background should have access to a comprehensive presentation of Jewish history.

My grandfather owned, or could borrow, books of Jewish ethical content. *Pirkei Avot (Ethics of the Fathers)* with Ladino translation was a favorite of his. He had access to the Ladino translation of *Hovot ha-Levavot (Duties of the Heart)*, by the great medieval Sephardic pietist Bahya ibn Pakuda. He also owned a copy of a lengthy Ladino poem about Joseph and his brothers. This poem, which he read to his family as a form of storytelling entertainment, was obviously imbued with moral lessons.

Another standard work found in Sephardic home libraries was the *Zohar*, the classic volume of Kabbalah. Although my grandfather could read the Aramaic words easily enough, he was not trained in kabbalistic teachings. Yet, he knew the *Zohar* was a sacred text that contained deep truths and mysteries.

My grandfather subscribed to the Ladino weekly newspapers of his time, *La America* (1910–25) and *La Vara* (1922–48). These papers provided news of the world, of the Jewish communities in the old countries, of Jewish life in America, and other features, including poetry, Ladino songs and proverbs, opinion pieces, and humor. He would read the newspapers to his wife and children, to keep them informed and entertained. He also owned several novels in Ladino, and these too would be read to the family for their pleasure.

This modest library contained the essential ingredients of Sephardic civilization: the Biblical and rabbinic traditions, Jewish law and ethics, Kabbalah, folklore, history, and literature. Jewish source texts were translated and interpreted through the medium of Judeo-Spanish culture.

It should not be imagined that my grandparents were part of a tiny, exotic community, representatives of a frail stream within Jewry. On the contrary, the Judeo-Spanish tradition had flourished for centuries, had created a vast literature, and was a significant part of world Jewry.

In the early years of the twentieth century, well over four hundred thousand Jews lived in the Ottoman Empire—the fifth largest Jewish community in the world at that time.[16] While over one hundred thousand of Ottoman Jews were Arabic speakers who lived in the Middle East, almost all of the Jews of Turkey and the Balkan countries—the heartland of the Ottoman Empire—were native speakers of Judeo-Spanish. Thousands of Jews of Judeo-Spanish background were to be found in the Land of Israel (then part of the Ottoman Empire), the United States, Europe, Latin America, and in a few enclaves in Africa. Thus, the Judeo-Spanish community was composed of a substantial population, centered in Turkey and with outposts throughout the world. There were, of course, other Jews who lived in the Ottoman Empire, as well as other Sephardim who did not live in Turkey and the Balkans. In this book, though, when I refer to Ottoman Jewry or Sephardic Jewry, I am referring specifically to this group of Jews of Judeo-Spanish culture.

Although linked by a shared language, culture, and historical memory, it was not a monolithic group. By the early twentieth century, the Sephardim had undergone several generations of "modernization" and "westernization." Their traditional culture was in the throes of radical change.

The Judeo-Spanish civilization of the Ottoman Empire began with the arrival of Sephardic Jews in the late fifteenth century, following the cruel expulsion of Jews from Spain in 1492. So let us start our story from the beginning.

2

Iberian Roots

The Sephardic presence in the Ottoman Empire is popularly dated from 1492, when thousands of Jewish exiles from Spain found haven in the domains of Sultan Bayezid II (r. 1481–1512). In 1992, the Jews of Turkey sponsored elaborate programs and celebrations to mark the quincentennial anniversary and to express appreciation to Turkey for having provided a home to its Jewish population. The quincentennial committee followed the precedent established a century earlier, when the Jews of Turkey commemorated their four-hundredth anniversary with much fanfare. These events emphasized the theme that the Turkish Empire had been benevolent, tolerant, and hospitable to the Jews. Turkish kindness was contrasted with the cruelty the Jews had suffered at the hands of the fanatical Catholic monarchs of Spain, Ferdinand and Isabella.

While it is true that Sephardic culture became dominant after 1492, Jewish communities existed in the empire well before the arrival of the Jewish exiles from Spain. The earlier communities were part of the Eastern Roman Empire. Most were Romaniot Jews, who spoke Greek and followed the Jewish rite known as *minhag Romania.*

During the first half of the fifteenth century, a Jew in Turkey wrote a letter to his coreligionists living in Christian lands. The writer, Yitzhak Zarfaty, described himself as a French Jew who had been born in Germany and had settled in Edirne. In his letter, he contrasted the excellent conditions enjoyed by Jews in the Ottoman Empire with the terrible afflictions "more bitter than death that have befallen our brethren in Germany." He proclaimed:

> Turkey is a land wherein nothing is lacking, and where, if you will, all shall yet be well with you. The way to the Holy Land lies open to you through Turkey. Is it not better for you to live under Muslims than under Christians? Here every man may dwell at peace under his own vine and fig tree. Here you are allowed to wear the most precious garments.[1]

The situation described in Zarfaty's letter found a receptive audience among some of the Jews in Europe. Even before 1492, Jews from Germany, France, and Spain were moving to the more congenial domains of Turkey. But, clearly, a major turning point for Jewish life in Turkey occurred with the influx of Spanish Jews in 1492 and thereafter.

The Expulsion of Jews from Spain

When King Ferdinand and Queen Isabella decreed the expulsion of Jews from Spain in the spring of 1492, this culminated over a thousand years of Jewish life there. During their centuries in Spain, Jews had known good times and bad; their situation fluctuated depending on a variety of factors—prime among them, the level of religious fanaticism or tolerance of Spain's rulers.

Jews had been persecuted and forcibly converted by the early Christian rulers of Spain, and therefore welcomed the Muslim conquest of much of Spain early in the eighth century. Indeed, Jewish life began to flourish under Muslim rule. The tenth and eleventh centuries witnessed a remarkable flowering of Jewish intellectual life, with Spanish Jews making classic contributions to rabbinic literature, Hebrew poetry, biblical studies, grammar, philosophy, and ethics. They also made significant contributions to science, mathematics, medicine, finance, and political life. In short, the Jews of Spain were active participants in their society.

The period of the Christian reconquest of Spain was initiated early in the eleventh century. The Jews who came under Christian rule during the eleventh and twelfth centuries still flourished. By the early thirteenth century, though, Jewish life in Christian Spain took a turn for the worse. Jews were subjected to a variety of legal disabilities. Anti-Jewish sentiment increased among the Christian populace. The kingdom of Aragon undertook a campaign to convert Jews to Christianity, with fanatical Christian clerics fanning the flames of hatred and violence against Jews. Public disputations were staged in order to humiliate Jews and Judaism.

In 1391, anti-Jewish riots broke out throughout Christian Spain, resulting in the murder of many Jews. Jewish property was destroyed; synagogues were confiscated and converted into churches. During this period of persecution, thousands of Jews converted to Christianity under duress in order to save their lives, their homes, and their businesses.

When Aragon and Castile were united in 1479, Ferdinand and Isabella wished to consolidate their joint kingdom as a Catholic domain. In 1480, two Dominicans were named inquisitors for the kingdom of Castile, in order to hunt down Jewish converts to Christianity who still maintained Jewish religious practices. A number of conversos (Jews who had converted to Catholicism) were tortured and burned at the stake. In 1481, inquisitors were appointed for Aragon. In 1483, Jews were expelled from Andalusia. In January 1492, Christian forces conquered Granada, the last Muslim stronghold in Spain. A few months later, in April, the king and queen issued their infamous decree expelling Jews from their kingdom. Jews were given several months to settle their affairs and leave the country. Those who converted to Christianity—and many thousands did—were allowed to remain, but had to live under the menacing eye of the Inquisition.

Rabbi Yitzhak Abravanel, the preeminent Jewish leader at the time of the expulsion, estimated that three hundred thousand Jews left Spain. While this number is merely an estimate, it indicates that a large number of Jews chose to leave Spain rather than forsake their religion.

Rabbi Abravanel's comments illustrate the depth of the tragedy that overwhelmed Spanish Jewry, but also the profound faith of those Jews who left Spain:

> This was the exile of Jerusalem which was in Spain where the people had dwelled in the land of their sojourning with honor, resting in their place.... From the rising of the sun to its setting, from north to south, there was never such a chosen people [as the Jews of Spain] in beauty and pleasantness; and afterwards, there will never be another such people. God was with them, the children of Judea and Jerusalem, many and strong. [They were] a quiet and trusting people, a people filled with the blessing of God with no end to its treasures; a pure and upright people, revering the Lord. I am the man who saw this people in its glory, in its beauty, in its pleasantness.[2]

Although Abravanel and other Jewish leaders strove to have the expulsion decree rescinded, they did not succeed. Ominously, the date of the expulsion corresponded to the Jewish month of Av, during the season of the Fast of Av. This saddest date on the Jewish calendar commemorates the destruction of both the First and Second Temples in ancient Jerusalem. Now the expulsion of Spanish Jewry was to be linked forever to this day of fasting and mourning.

Rabbi Abravanel recorded the reaction of Jews to the expulsion edict:

> The people heard this evil decree and they mourned. Wherever word of the decree reached, there was great mourning among the Jews. There was great trembling and

sorrow the likes of which had not been experienced since the days of the exile of Jews from their land to the land of foreigners. The Jews encouraged each other: let us strengthen ourselves on behalf of our faith, on behalf of the Torah of our God…. If [our enemies] let us live, we will live; and if they murder us, we will die. But we will not profane our covenant [with God], and our hearts will not retrogress; we will walk forward in the name of the Lord our God.[3]

The exiles suffered physical and spiritual hardships. Some were sold into slavery; others were murdered by ruthless ship captains. They suffered from diseases, hunger and thirst, physical exhaustion. Families were separated, with some family members choosing to leave the Iberian Peninsula as Jews and others choosing to accept Catholicism rather than go into exile. The Jews wondered why this terrible tragedy had befallen them, why God had let it come to pass.[4]

Many Spanish Jews crossed the border into Portugal. However, when Judaism was outlawed in Portugal in 1497, open Jewish life in the Iberian Peninsula came to an end.

Some Spanish and Portuguese Jews sought haven in the cities of Italy and other locations in western Europe. Catholic lands, though, were not particularly hospitable to Jews in that age of religious fanaticism. Others resettled in North Africa. Some reestablished their lives in the Land of Israel.

A large contingent of Sephardic exiles migrated to the mighty and relatively benevolent Ottoman Empire. Major centers of Sephardic Jewry emerged in Istanbul and Salonika, with many other sizeable communities developing in the southern Balkans and western Anatolia. Among the larger communities were Patras, Thebes, Trikkala, Edirne, Valona, and Bursa. A thriving community developed in Rhodes beginning in 1523, after the Ottoman Empire conquered the island from the Knights of St. John. A large community also emerged in the seventeenth century in Izmir. Smaller Jewish communities, many of them dominated by the incoming Sephardic exiles, could be found in many cities and towns of the Ottoman Empire.[5]

Sephardic Predominance

With the influx of Sephardic Jews into Turkey, the fabric of local Jewish life underwent a period of transition. While the Romaniot Jews certainly assisted the Sephardic refugees, they also harbored some resentment over the growing influence of Sephardim in community life. Tensions arose not just in the social sphere, but in matters of Jewish law and custom. Differences in language, liturgy, and halakhic practice created problems between the groups.[6] Rabbi Moshe Capsali of Istanbul was not alone among Romaniot leaders in wanting to maintain Romaniot traditions in the face of pressure by the Sephardic newcomers. He urged his fellow Romaniot Jews of Candia to resist the efforts of newly arrived Sephardim to change the customs of the native community. He noted that Candia's Jews had long followed the legal rulings of the Franco-German Tosafists, particularly those of Rabbeinu Yaacov Tam (1100–1171). The Sephardim preferred the rulings of their own Spanish rabbis.[7]

The Sephardim assumed that they would take control of the Jewish communities in which they settled. Although they were refugees, they did not lose their sense of pride and nobility. They knew that they brought with them the peerless traditions of Sephardic Jewry—and they expected the local non-Sephardic Jews to defer to them. A Sephardic rabbi of Salonika, writing in 1509, addressed the following words to the leaders of the Jewish community in Edirne:

> It is well known that Sephardic Jews and their sages in this kingdom, together with other congregations who join them, comprise the majority here, may the Lord be praised. The land was given uniquely to them, and they are its majesty, its radiance and splendor, a light unto the land and

unto all who dwell in it. Surely, they were not brought hither in order to depart! For all these places are ours too, and it would be worthy of all the minority peoples who first resided in this kingdom [the Romaniots] to follow their example and do as they do in all that pertains to the Torah and its customs.[8]

Rabbi Shemuel de Medina, one of the great rabbinic luminaries of sixteenth-century Salonika, was asked about the right of the majority Sephardim to impose their rite of prayer on the minority of non-Sephardim. The query indicates that with the arrival of Sephardim in Salonika

almost everyone has changed to the Sephardic form of prayer, since they are the majority in this kingdom, and their prayers are clear and sweet. All or most have abandoned their customs and have been drawn to follow the Sephardic custom, as it is today in Salonika, where the congregations of Calabria, Provence, Sicily and Apulia have adopted the Sephardic rite. The Ashkenazic congregation is the only one that has not changed its custom [to that of the Sephardim].[9]

In his reply, Rabbi de Medina praised those who gave up their particular rites in order to follow the Sephardic rite—which he was convinced was the best.

When the Sephardim arrived in the cities and towns of the Ottoman Empire, they themselves were hardly a monolithic group. They tended to form congregations on the basis of their cities of origin in Spain and Portugal. Istanbul and Salonika, as prime examples, had numerous Sephardic synagogues based on the members' towns of origin in the Iberian Peninsula.[10] The historian Joseph Nehama offers a colorful description of Sephardim who settled in Salonika, pointing out their differing cultural characteristics:

The Aragonese and the Catalonians, although they traveled together, did not mingle at all with each other. From the very beginning they separated into two communities, very different from each other. The Aragonese, who had lived in the interior of Spain, were adherents of the past, traditionalists, suspicious of their independence, rights and privileges, and at the same time instinctively domineering, proud to excess, on the border of stubbornness, often sulky, cold, self-centered, somber, and almost taciturn, rough in manners, of an exaggerated circumspection and of a rugged and meticulous honesty. The Aragonese were little prone to exert much effort and little inclined to work; indeed they were lazy and apathetic. The Catalonians, on the other hand, were a people from the seacoast, alert and mobile, friends of novelty, gay, communicative, of smooth and polished manners, of vivid intelligence, penetrating in their enterprises, self-willed in their projects; the Catalonians were all activity, exuberant in their vitality. Skillful in their work, the Jews hailing from Barcelona, Gerona, Tarragona and from the Valencian coasts were hard workers, unrelenting in their industry. *Los Catalanes de las piedras sacan panes*, the Catalonians are capable of getting bread out of the very stones. [The Sephardim from Galicia] spoke loud and had great difficulty in being understood by the Castilians, Aragonese and Catalonians. The Gallegos were not numerous enough to form a community of their own. A little while after their arrival, they were assimilated with the immigrants from Lisbon whom they most resembled linguistically.[11]

Yet, in spite of the internal differences and tensions among the Sephardic Jews, they gradually melded into a relatively homogeneous culture. There may have been variations in custom from community to community, particular pride in the communities from which they stemmed in the Iberian Peninsula, and differences in pronunciation of Spanish. Within a generation or two, though, these differences were not as sharp or troublesome as they were in the years right after 1492. The Sephardim as a group achieved a high degree of cultural supremacy in the communities in which they settled.

The success of the Sephardim did not arise simply because they thought themselves to be superior to the local Jews. In point of fact, they *were* superior in various ways. Notably, their numbers included outstanding rabbinic scholars, as well as a laity that was versed in Jewish law and lore. Rabbi Yosef Mitrani of Istanbul observed that the study of Torah flourished throughout the Ottoman Empire, North Africa, and the Holy Land

> by virtue of the sages of Castile who came from there and established study in all these lands, and from whose efforts we benefit today. In Galilee [Safed] people would say: Let us be grateful to the rulers of Spain for having expelled our sages and judges, so that they came here and re-established the Torah in all its pristine glory....[12]

Sephardic sages taught their communities in their Spanish vernacular. Their goal was to create broad frameworks for study and instruction using efficient teaching methods.[13] An Arabic-speaking rabbi of sixteenth-century Safed, Rabbi Issakhar ibn Sussan the Magrebi, noted that the Spanish rabbis taught in Ladino, rather than in Hebrew. Thus, they were able to reach all segments of the community, not only the rabbinic elite.[14]

The Sephardic arrivals in the Ottoman Empire were quick to establish synagogues, schools, and yeshivot for advanced Torah studies. They opened publishing houses to produce books of Jewish learning. Wealthy patrons supported the publication of rabbinic works.

Professor Joseph Hacker has pointed out that Sephardic dominance was the result of various factors. The Sephardic immigrants brought with them their "ancestral spiritual possessions"—the heritage of intellectual achievement in Spain. They brought books and manuscripts. The resettlement period in the Ottoman Empire was characterized by intellectual ferment among the Sephardic newcomers who had come from different cities in Iberia.

Surely, the Romaniot Jews had outstanding rabbis and scholars, such as Rabbis Eliyahu Mizrahi and Moshe Capsali; yet the Sephardim were able to predominate due to their greater numbers and their larger circle of educated laity. Moreover, when the Ottoman rulers moved many Romaniot Jews to Istanbul following the conquest of 1453, this depleted the communities from which the Romaniots had been deported. When Sephardim came to these towns, there was little or no indigenous Jewish population to resist Sephardic control.[15]

Another vital factor was "the well-developed self-awareness of the Jews of Castile, Aragon, Catalonia, Navarre and Portugal." These exiles arrived with a clear sense of mission: to renew the Jewish culture they had enjoyed in their homeland. In Professor Hacker's words:

> The fear of [their Jewish tradition] vanishing, on the one hand, and their unquestioned faith in its importance and supremacy, on the other, were central factors in their motivation and their drive to write and to print, so as to preserve it and revitalize it. Both scholars and simple folk felt that their sacrifice in leaving the Iberian peninsula would be pointless—the dangers they suffered and the financial losses they absorbed—were their heritage and faith to disappear off the face of the earth, or even fade and be absorbed in other traditions.[16]

Added to these factors was their feeling of cultural superiority that impacted on the social and religious dynamics of the communities in which they settled.

Aside from their predominance in Jewish learning and communal institutional life, the Sephardic immigrants were successful

in worldly matters as well. Sephardic physicians were highly
regarded, having brought with them advanced European medical
knowledge. They became doctors to the sultans and high-ranking
dignitaries. As trusted advisers to Turkish rulers, these Jewish doctors were able to intercede on behalf of the Jewish community in
times of crisis.[17] Salonika became an important medical and scien-
tific center with the arrival in 1558 of Amatus Lusitanus (1511–68),
an outstanding converso physician who was one of Europe's most
renowned medical authorities. Born in Portugal as Joao Rodrigues,
he studied medicine at the University of Salamanca in Spain, later
teaching at the University of Ferrara. In Salonika, he returned to
Judaism with the Hebrew name Haviv ha-Sefardi. He trained other
doctors and gathered around him a group of scientists and
philosophers.[18]

Jews were active in local commerce, importing and exporting,
and tax farming. They were pioneers in the Ottoman textile industry, creating manufacturing centers in Salonika and Safed, as well
as participating actively in this industry in Istanbul and other
urban centers. Jews worked as goldsmiths, silversmiths, and dealers
in precious stones; they were active in the production and trade of
soap, perfumes, and spices, as well as in many other crafts and
trades. They held important positions in the customs offices and
mints of Turkey and also developed a significant business relationship with the corps of Janissaries.[19] The Janissaries were an elite
unit of Turkish infantry. This group came into existence in the
fourteenth century and served as the sultan's guard until 1826,
when the sultan disbanded the Janissary Corps. Indeed, the Jewish
exiles from Spain were such a productive and enterprising group
that the sultan was reported to have said that the king of Spain
must be a fool for having enriched the Ottoman Empire at the
expense of his own kingdom.[20]

Jews also brought skills in weaponry and related technology
that may have proved valuable to the already proficient Turkish
military establishment. Some Spanish Jews were involved in arms
production and brought their skills and knowledge to Turkey. A

Spanish Christian visitor, writing in the mid-sixteenth century, thought that the Jews had given Turkey military advantages that could be used against Europe:

> Here at Constantinople are many Jews, descendants of those whom the Catholic King Don Ferdinand ordered to be driven forth of Spain, and would that it had pleased God that they be drowned in the sea in coming hither! For they taught our enemies the most of what they know of the villainies of war, such as the use of brass ordnance and of firelocks.[21]

The phenomenal rise of Don Joseph Nasi and his aunt Doña Gracia Mendes was the most dramatic Jewish success story in sixteenth-century Turkey. Having been conversos in Portugal, they returned to Judaism in Turkey and established a great international banking and trading house. The sultan thought so highly of Nasi that he appointed him Duke of Naxos—a rare honor to be given to a non-Muslim. Don Joseph, Doña Gracia, and other Jews of the financial elite were influential in strengthening the Jewish position in the Ottoman Empire.

Jewish traders maintained business relationships with Jews in other lands. Conversos who returned to Judaism in the Ottoman Empire were particularly active in international trade. By the mid-sixteenth century, Jews had become so prominent in the Ottoman economy that a Christian traveler, Pierre Bellon, claimed that Jews "have taken over the traffic and commerce of Turkey to such an extent that the Turk's wealth and revenue is in their hands."[22] While this is very likely an exaggerated statement, it nevertheless points to the prominence of Jews in Turkish economic life. Since so many of these Jews were Sephardim, it was inevitable that their financial success should impact on the communal and cultural dynamics within the Jewish community.

While many Jews did achieve financial success, many others— probably the majority—were of modest means or actually poor.

Economic opportunities varied from person to person, from city to city. Yet, the Jewish community as a whole prospered, and the wealthier members were able to help their needy coreligionists and support the Jewish communal institutions.[23]

The Predominance of the Spanish Language

A clear indication of the cultural hegemony of the Sephardim was the gradual predominance of their language among non-Sephardic Jews. This was true in much of Turkey, the Balkan countries, and in the Land of Israel. A number of communities in Greece, though, continued to maintain Greek as their spoken language. In those few communities, the Spanish-speaking Jews eventually dropped Spanish and adopted Greek. Moreover, in the Arabic-speaking provinces of the Ottoman Empire, the Sephardim gradually became absorbed into the local Arabic-speaking Jewish communities.

Although the Sephardim spoke different dialects in the Iberian Peninsula, once they arrived in the Ottoman Empire it was the Castilian Spanish that gained ascendancy. Joseph Nehama described the phenomenon:

> But above the dialects and the jargons dominates the Castilian language, known by the majority of these men, almost all of them cultured and often remarkably well versed in belles lettres. For communal acts, for announcements, for sermons, for business transactions, for the inter-relationship among the people of the different provinces, they have recourse to Castilian…. The haughty Castilians contemplated this rapid triumph with great pleasure. Is there in the whole world, according to their view, a more harmonious and nobler language than theirs? Castilian enjoys the highest prestige in all Spain, where a cohort of writers and scholars, encouraged by the princes, have raised it to literary dignity.[24]

Within a generation or two, the non-Sephardic Jews of Istanbul, Salonika, Edirne, Rhodes, and many other communities were using Spanish as their mother tongue. While differences in pronunciation and usage continued to exist among the various communities, a shared Judeo-Spanish culture had emerged by the mid-sixteenth century.[25] Elements of the minority Jewish traditions were incorporated into the Judeo-Spanish language and lifestyle, as were aspects of the languages and traditions of the people among whom the Jews lived. Thus, the Judeo-Spanish language— while essentially Spanish—also included words and phrases drawn from Hebrew, Turkish, Greek, and other languages and later also came to include vocabulary drawn from French, Italian, and other European languages.

Family Names

The family names of Sephardim of Judeo-Spanish background provide an interesting insight into the multicultural background of Jews of the Ottoman Empire. Some names reflect Iberian cities of origin: Toledo, Toledano, Cordova, Cordovero, de Jaen, de Leon, Muscatel, Soriano, Navarro, Taragano. Other names stem back to Jewish families of medieval Spain: Maimon, Benveniste, Benadrete, Aboab, Aboulafia, Abravanel. Some names reflect Spanish nomenclature: Angel, Calderon, Varon, Pinto, Ventura.

Among Judeo-Spanish-speaking Jews, a number of family names indicate non-Sephardic origins. Individuals of various backgrounds were absorbed into the Sephardic community and became integral parts of it. A well-known name among Sephardim is Ashkenazy or Eskenazi, that is, German/Ashkenazic. The original members of the family were Ashkenazic Jews who were identified as Ashkenazim by the larger Sephardic community. In referring to individuals as such, these adjectives were transformed into family names. This process applied to Jews from other origins as well: Sarfaty (from France); Franco (from Europe); Romey (from Romaniot/Greek background).

The first names of Jews also indicated a blend of cultures and civilizations that had melded into the Judeo-Spanish tradition. Some of these names reflected non-Judeo-Spanish traditions of the Jews of the Ottoman Empire, including Turkish influence. While most first names were of Hebrew and biblical origin, Spanish names were also evident: Gracia, Vida, Estrella, Luna, Stella, Salvador, Mercado, Leon. Some names were drawn from the Turkish and Arabic: Sultana, Kadun, Misodi, Zimbul, Chelibi, Saadya. Names were also taken from Greek, and later from French and other European languages: Calo, Eugenie, Victoria, Regina, Moise, Victor.

While Judeo-Spanish civilization was influenced by other traditions, it basically "Hispanized" these traditions and incorporated them into the Sephardic culture.

The Conversos

The Jews who departed from Spain in 1492 left as professing Jews. When they established homes in new lands, they reorganized their lives while following the laws and customs of their religion. The Spanish they spoke was that of the fifteenth century. As generations passed, they continued to speak Spanish—but in isolation from Spain. The Spanish language in Spain underwent natural development, but the Spanish of the Jews in Turkey essentially remained "medieval."

During the sixteenth and seventeenth centuries, the Judeo-Spanish communities were reinforced by the arrival of a steady stream of conversos—Jews who had converted (or whose ancestors had converted) to Catholicism rather than leave Spain in 1492 or Portugal in 1497. The conversos who returned to Judaism in the Ottoman Empire integrated themselves into the flourishing Sephardic communities. At the same time, they brought with them the Spanish language as it had developed in Spain to the time of their departure. Thus, the Ottoman Judeo-Spanish communities could revitalize their Spanish language in light of the language brought in by the newcomers from Spain and Portugal.

Professor Benardete has referred to the original Sephardic exiles of 1492 as "medieval Jews." For the most part, the intellectual and cultural baggage they brought with them was from medieval Spain. On the other hand, Benardete suggests, the conversos who arrived from Spain over the next several centuries were "renaissance Jews." They brought not only an updated Spanish language, but also updated European knowledge and attitudes.[26] As long as these renaissance Jews were interacting with the medieval Jews, the Jewish communities enjoyed the benefit of revitalization of language and ideas. By the end of the seventeenth century, though, the influx of conversos had dried up. From then on, Judeo-Spanish civilization was on its own, without any significant contact or interchange with Spain.

By the late sixteenth century, Amsterdam had become a center of return to Judaism for ex-conversos.[27] This group of renaissance Jews did indeed enjoy much success in the communities in which they settled in Europe and the New World. Although these returning Jews continued to speak Spanish and Portuguese for a number of generations, they also learned the languages of the cities in which they lived. By the middle of the eighteenth century, Spanish and Portuguese had almost completely died out as living tongues among the descendants of the conversos in Europe and America.

Yet, the Jews in the Ottoman Empire maintained Judeo-Spanish as their mother tongue into the twentieth century. Few of them could even speak Turkish. In 1840, the chief rabbi of Istanbul, Rabbi Hayyim Moshe Fresco, issued a circular letter in Ladino calling on the Jews throughout the Ottoman Empire to study the Turkish language. This letter, though, had little if any effect. The Jews continued to speak their own language, rather than learn Turkish.

Why would Sephardic Jews of the Ottoman Empire continue to speak Judeo-Spanish rather than learn Turkish and thereby integrate more successfully into the Turkish society? While their renaissance Sephardic brethren were learning Dutch, French, and

English and adapting to their new lands, the medieval Sephardim preferred to remain "medieval," linguistically isolated from the Turkish-speaking society in which they lived.

One of the reasons for this phenomenon may be that the Sephardim of the Ottoman Empire simply thought of their culture as being superior to that of their non-Jewish neighbors. They felt no need to emulate others or to integrate into the Turkish cultural milieu. They did not see themselves—nor were they seen by the non-Jews—as permanent "citizens" of the Ottoman Empire. Rather, they were outsiders to Turkish life. It was not until the mid-nineteenth century that the Ottoman government exerted serious efforts to make Jews feel like equal citizens of the empire—and these efforts were only minimally successful. So the Jews maintained their own language and social structure for over four centuries; they lived in the empire, but were not entirely incorporated into it.

The conversos who returned to Judaism in western Europe, on the other hand, came to see their futures as being tied to the countries in which they lived. They adopted the European languages and mores and ultimately strove for acceptance and political equality in their new lands. They admired the surrounding culture and wanted to be part of it. They dropped their Iberian languages, thinking them unnecessary for their goal of becoming part of their new societies.

The medieval Jews, then, were the ones who had the mindset and social conditions necessary to maintain their traditional language over the centuries. Although they were expelled from Spain, they did not drop their Spanish language and attitudes. Although they were living in the Ottoman Empire, they did not stop thinking of themselves as Spanish Jews, with a distinctive Jewish and Hispanic culture.

Leon Sciaky, a twentieth-century writer from Salonika, described the Sephardic mystique of his hometown in words that equally could be applied to the other Judeo-Spanish communities of the Ottoman Empire. About the Sephardim, he wrote:

Their dignity, their fastidious appearance, their mellow, fluent Castilian or Portuguese were part of the greatness of their country, in the life of which they had for centuries played so prominent a part, and to whose culture and wealth they had fully contributed.... Free and unhindered in their new environment, the Jews of Turkey, and especially of Salonika, retained their Spanish character, in their customs, in their cooking, in their social amenities, and in their pride and dignity.[28]

Although the Sephardim did indeed maintain a Hispanic culture and character, they did not live in a vacuum. The Ottoman experience was a powerful factor in the development of Judeo-Spanish civilization. We turn now to a discussion of the role of the Ottoman Empire in the life and culture of the Sephardim.

3

The Ottoman Milieu

The Jewish exiles from fifteenth-century Iberia had been accustomed to living in a Spanish-speaking, Catholic-ruled, European society. When they arrived in the Ottoman Empire, they found themselves in a Turkish-speaking, Islamic-ruled, non-western society. On the one hand, they wanted to maintain the way of life that they had brought with them from Spain and Portugal; on the other hand, they needed to adapt to conditions in their new land of residence.

The Ottoman Empire dated back to 1299, founded by Osman I. Centered around the borders of the Mediterranean Sea, the empire reached its height during the sixteenth century. It included Anatolia, much of the Middle East, parts of North Africa, and much of southeastern Europe to the Caucasus in the north. The Ottoman Empire came to an end in 1922, with modern Turkey emerging as its immediate successor state.

We have described how the Sephardic arrivals came to predominate in the life of the Jewish communities of Turkey and the Balkan countries. In matters of internal Jewish life, the Sephardic patterns brought from the Iberian Peninsula were successfully transplanted. Yet, the Jews had to relate to the Ottoman government, the Muslim society, and the Christian minorities—especially Greeks and Armenians. These relationships obviously had an impact on their lives. How did the early Sephardic arrivals view their new situation in the Ottoman Empire?

A number of sixteenth-century Jewish writers described the position of Jews in Ottoman society in laudatory terms. The historian Samuel Usque was extravagant in his praise of the religious freedom enjoyed by Ottoman Jewry and thanked God for this blessing. He referred to Salonika as "the mother of Judaism," since that community conducted itself "based on the most profound elements of the Torah."[1] Another writer thanked the Almighty, who "in His mercy has had us find favor with all the gentiles amongst whom we dwell, so that we are almost known here by a new name: the redeemed of God—so light is the Turkish yoke upon us."[2] Rabbi Simhah Luzzatto of Venice noted:

> The main center of the [Jewish] nation is in the land of the Turkish sultan, not merely because Jews have always been dwelling there but also because Jewish émigrés from Spain hastened there, a large number of these finally arriving in the lands of that state. The reason for this was, first of all, that there they were granted freedom to observe their religion, in light of the tolerance the Turks normally show to faiths other than their own; there are also a great many Greeks there, who observe other customs, so that the Turks pay no attention to the religion and customs of the Jews.[3]

Ottoman Jews fostered the notion that the Sultan Mehmed (who ruled 1451–81, including the time of the Ottoman conquest of Constantinople in 1453) was favorably disposed to the Jews— and actually studied the Hebrew language. He was said to have been on close terms with Istanbul's Rabbi Moshe Capsali and other Jewish dignitaries, and that he even enjoyed eating kosher food and participating in a Passover Seder.[4] These Jewish "foundation myths" were akin to the traditions maintained by Greeks and Armenians—that Mehmed had shown special favoritism to them. These myths were important to minorities, who could then use these traditions in their dealings with later sultans: since Mehmed himself favored us, it would be appropriate for you to follow his example.

Eliyahu Capsali, a doctor and author living in Candia, reflected the Jewish enthusiasm for Turkish rule when he described Sultan Suleyman the Magnificent's conquest of the Island of Rhodes. Capsali viewed the Turkish victory as part of the messianic drama leading to redemption. He described Rhodes as the bride and Suleyman as the groom. Of Suleyman he wrote: "Your descendants shall inherit the cities of their enemies with joy and happiness. And your name in Israel will be known as Groom and Bride."[5]

With the Ottoman conquest of the Land of Israel in 1516, the Holy Land now became more accessible to Jewish pilgrims and to those who wished to settle there. When Suleyman the Magnificent rebuilt the walls of Jerusalem between 1536 and 1542, he won enthusiastic appreciation from Jews, further strengthening their messianic expectations.

The Jewish praises of the Ottoman Empire during the sixteenth century were, however, preceded by some negative attitudes during the fifteenth century. After the Ottomans conquered Constantinople in 1453, they repopulated the city by transferring people from various places in the empire. This forced movement of population, which included Jews from many towns in Turkey and the Balkans, naturally entailed resentment and hardship on the part of those who were relocated. Due to the forced population transfers, only a small number of Jews remained in the Ottoman Balkans within a few years after 1453; and twenty to thirty Jewish communities in Anatolia and Rumelia were transplanted intact to Istanbul. As Dr. Joseph Hacker has noted:

> The deportation and resettlement in Constantinople drew the deepest criticism and for good reason. The outcome of the forced deportations was very grave for Byzantine Jewry. Small in numbers before, now they were plagued and suffered from an economic and cultural crisis.[6]

Mehmed II did try to assuage the ill will of those who were forcibly transferred to Istanbul. He adopted policies toward non-Muslims that encouraged their economic and social development. His successor, Bayezid II, who ruled 1481–1512, imposed some severe restrictions on the Jews, but his negative actions were outweighed in the Jewish mind by his willingness to receive thousands of Spanish and Portuguese Jewish exiles into his empire. Later Jewish writers, then, could point to positive policies of Mehmed as well as Bayezid's reception of Sephardic Jews; these features tended to overshadow memories of the more negative aspects of the rules of Mehmed and Bayezid.[7]

The Status of Jews in Islamic Society

Islamic law provides full civil rights and privileges only to Muslims. Idolaters, that is, those who do not possess divinely revealed scriptures, are forced to accept Islam or face death. Jews and Christians—known as People of Scriptures—are tolerated as infidels and are subject to the laws of *dhimma*—protected people.

Dhimmis were generally granted religious autonomy and were allowed to conduct their lives according to their own religious traditions and authorities. They were granted toleration and protection upon payment of a special tax. They were also required to acknowledge the superior status of Muslims. Although *dhimmis* could own property and practice their religion freely, they were not allowed to build new houses of worship. This latter rule was often ignored by Muslim authorities, but there were times and places when the spirit of intolerance led to the closing of these buildings.

Dhimmis suffered from legal disabilities. Their evidence was not accepted against the evidence of a Muslim. A Muslim could not be executed for murdering a *dhimmi*. *Dhimmis* were not allowed to ride horseback or to carry weapons. Their right to travel freely was periodically restricted. Although some Christians and Jews rose to positions of influence in Muslim governments, these achievements were exceptions to the rule and depended on local situations and attitudes.

Non-Muslims were expected to wear distinctive clothing, although the exact requirements varied from place to place and era to era. Professor S. D. Goitein has pointed out: "The yellow badge for Jews was known in Muslim countries many centuries before it was introduced into Christian Europe."[8] A seventeenth-century observer remarked:

> The Jews in Turkey dress like the Turks except that they may not wear green, nor a white turban, nor a red jacket. They are usually dressed in violet but they are obliged to wear a violet bonnet made in the shape of and the same height as a hat, and those who have the means to own a turban wear it round the base of their bonnet. They must also wear socks and violet slippers.[9]

Professor Bernard Lewis, in studying the status of *dhimmis* in Muslim law and society, observed that "in contrast to Christian anti-Semitism, the Muslim attitude toward non-Muslims is one not of hate, fear or envy but simply of contempt. The language of abuse towards non-Muslims is often quite strong."[10]

Dr. Lewis noted that a common feature of all the Muslim regulations relating to *dhimmis* was "the concern to maintain and more especially to symbolize the social inferiority of the *dhimmis*, and the corresponding superiority of the Muslims."[11]

In his study of Jews in Jerusalem during the sixteenth century, Dr. Amnon Cohen also noted that the Jews suffered from little overt or doctrinal anti-Semitism, but were rather subjected to oppressions and humiliations as part of the routine of life. "The Jews could not be disdained for being primitive, but were looked down upon for the very fact of their being Jewish."[12]

The Muslim attitude was based on their belief that theirs was the only true religion and that the Koran had eclipsed the Bible of the Jews and of the Christians. Although people of these older religions had received some partial divine truths, the Muslims believed that they had corrupted these truths and were now walking in spiritual darkness. Their obstinacy in clinging to these older religions was a source of bitter amazement to the Muslims: why didn't Jews and Christians recognize the truth of the Koran? Since they willingly chose to reject Islam, they deserved to be humiliated and oppressed.

While both Christians and Jews were protected as subservient people, Muslim tradition was more antipathetic to Jews than to Christians.[13] This was true not only in classic texts of Islam, but also in the popular attitudes of the Muslim public. When Muslims wished to insult each other or to discredit an idea, they would say that their antagonist was of Jewish ancestry or that his idea was a Jewish idea. This was deemed the worst possible insult. Disdain for Jews continued throughout the generations. A nineteenth-century observer of life in Egypt wrote:

> The Muslim hates no other religion as he hates that of the Jews…. Even now that all forms of political oppression have ceased, at a time when such great tolerance is shown to the Christian population, the Arabs still bear the same contemptuous hatred of the Jews. It is a commonplace occurrence, for example, for two Arabs reviling each other to call each other Ibn Yahudi (or son of a Jew) as the supreme insult…. It should be mentioned that in these cases, they pronounce the word Yahudi in a violent and contemptuous tone that would be hard to reproduce.[14]

The Sephardic Encounter with the Muslim Ottoman Empire

Considering the negative status of Jews in Islamic law and the disdain for Jews in popular Islamic culture, how did the Sephardic exiles adapt to their new situation? The answer, for the first generations after 1492, seems to have been, fairly well.

The Sephardic exiles, after all, had suffered brutal oppression in Catholic Spain and Portugal. By comparison, life under Ottoman

Islamic rule must have seemed a blessing. Whereas in Christian Europe Jews were subjected to oppression, humiliation, forced conversion, and expulsion, in the Islamic Ottoman Empire they were received with relative benevolence. They could practice their religion and conduct their lives in relative freedom.

Moreover, during the late fifteenth and early sixteenth centuries, the Ottoman Empire was at its peak. It was powerful militarily and had a growing economy. It viewed the incoming Sephardic exiles as an asset and preferred a policy of tolerance rather than a strict application of the harshest *dhimmi* laws. The Jews, to be sure, knew that they were a tolerated minority with certain legal disabilities, but in Christian lands, their situation had been far worse.

Not only were the Sephardic exiles tolerated upon their arrival in the Ottoman Empire, they were viewed as a loyal population. Whereas Greeks, Armenians, and other Christian minorities might be suspected of having territorial claims against the empire, this was not the case with the Jews. They were entirely dependent upon the empire, and their own interest was inextricably bound to the well-being of the empire. The sultans showed high honor to individual Jews, appointing them as their doctors and advisers, even, as mentioned earlier, appointing Joseph Nasi (1524–79) as the Duke of Naxos.

Another important factor was the organizational structure of the Ottoman government vis-à-vis its minorities. Although recent scholarship has called into question the exact nature of the *millet* system and its application (or non-application) to Christians and Jews, the fact was that the minorities did enjoy considerable autonomy.[15] The *millet* system entailed the establishment of communities along religious lines, where these communities enjoyed considerable autonomy. The *millets* maintained their own institutions, and members of the *millets* related primarily to their own internal leaders rather than to the Ottoman government. The Jewish community, for example, maintained its own synagogues, schools, and courts—all under the aegis of Jewish leaders, rabbinic and lay. Jews spoke their own language, had their own neighborhoods, published their own books, and made their own communal ordinances (*hascamot*). Even in matters of taxation, Jewish assessors and collectors were in charge. Those taxes that needed to be paid to the Ottoman government were remitted by Jewish officials on behalf of their communities. The individual Jew did not pay taxes directly to the government, nor did the government address itself to the individual for taxes. This arrangement continued well into the nineteenth century.

Thus, the Jews formed ethnic islands within the much larger population of Muslims and Christians. In their own communities, Jews could maintain their beliefs, attitudes, and traditions while retaining a psychological separation between themselves and the society around them.

Although Jews were spiritually and emotionally reinforced by living in their own communities, they nevertheless did have to face unpleasant realities in the outside world. Jews were, after all, a small minority in the places of their residence. (Salonika was a significant exception, where Jews actually formed the majority of the city's population during the sixteenth century and continued in that majority until the twentieth century.) While general Muslim attitudes toward Jews were quite negative, Christian attitudes were often worse—and more dangerous. Periodically, often at the season of Passover, Christians would accuse Jews of murdering Christians for ritual purposes. Although these vicious blood libels, as they were known, were patently false, gullible and hate-filled masses were quick to believe them, subjecting Jews to attack and murder. The Ottoman authorities generally tried to protect Jews from these Christian outrages. Jews preferred to live near Muslims rather than Christians, feeling that they could manage Muslim antipathy more easily than Christian hatred.

The Janissary Corps, with whom Jews did business, was also a source of trouble. Jews, along with other groups, suffered from predations from the Janissaries and other military units. Jews, who had little means of self-defense, seem to have been regarded as particularly easy targets.[16]

A Christian pilgrim, describing his travels in the early sixteenth century, catches an odd dilemma of Ottoman Jews. He
noted that the Jews were

> a people scattered throughout the whole world, and hated by
> those amongst whom they live; yet suffered as a necessary
> mischief; subject to all wrongs and contumelies, which they
> support with an invincible patience. Many of them have I
> seen abused; some of them beaten; yet never saw I a Jew with
> an angry countenance…. In general, they are worldly wise,
> and thrive wheresoever they set footing. The Turk employs
> them in receipts of customs, which they by their policies have
> enhanced, and in buying and selling with the Christians.[17]

Sephardic Jews had a strong sense of inner pride, a desire to
control the workings of the Jewish communities, a record of success and hard work in business. Yet, these Jewish *hidalgos* (Spanish
aristocrats) were subjected to humiliations and attacks by non-
Jews—and they accepted these insults with equanimity! They were
amazingly patient, even cheerful, in the face of these injustices
against them.

This stoicism might be explained in a number of ways. Jews
may have been reluctant to fight back against their oppressors for
fear of more widespread attacks against their community. They
were, after all, a tiny minority group who depended entirely on the
benevolence of others. They were not living in the Ottoman
Empire by right, but only as tolerated guests—who could be
expelled at the whim of the sultan. Recognizing their vulnerability,
the Jews felt that they were in no position to jeopardize themselves
by fighting with Muslims, or even with Christians.

Moreover, the Jews may well have viewed their oppressors as
despicable individuals, beneath contempt. There was no more
point in confronting such people than in fighting against mad
dogs. It was better to suffer the abuse quietly and get away from the
enemy as quickly as possible.

It should also be remembered that Jews had long been accustomed to being oppressed and deprived of rights. In no Christian or Muslim lands did Jews enjoy full civil rights, nor did they even expect to be treated fairly and justly. They interpreted their sufferings as being punishment for their sins, as part of God's divine plan; or as a stage in the process leading to the messianic era. In spite of the legal disabilities imposed on them, and in spite of the many difficulties and humiliations they suffered at the hands of Muslims and Christians, the Jews saw themselves as God's chosen people, destined to lead the world to messianic redemption and peace. Those who oppressed them would ultimately pay for their sins against the Jewish people.

We must now take a closer look at the religious ideas and practices that imbued the Sephardic communities in the generations after the expulsion from Spain. A study of their rich inner life will help us to understand how they coped with harsh external realities that confronted them.

4

Religious Foundations

The Jewish exiles from Spain and Portugal transplanted their way of life in their new homes in the Ottoman Empire. Although the expulsion from the Iberian Peninsula had caused them severe physical and emotional hardships, they brought with them a rich tradition that helped them to cope with their difficult situation. The Bible and the Talmud were the primary texts of their religious worldview, providing them inspiration as well as a practical framework for life. They drew also on the teachings of the great sages who had flourished in Spain during the medieval period.

Bible, Talmud, and Midrashim

The biblical tradition, along with the early rabbinic literature of the Talmud and midrashim, were the religious mainstays of the entire Jewish people. Jews could point with pride to the Hebrew Bible as a guiding light not just for Judaism, but for the daughter religions of Christianity and Islam. Although the later religions counted far more adherents and controlled greater worldly power, the Jews were strengthened by the fact that both of these later faiths acknowledged the sanctity of the Hebrew Bible. As the great medieval Sephardic poet and thinker Yehudah Halevy (c. 1075–1141) had made clear in his classic philosophical work *The Kuzari,* ultimate truth was to be found among the followers of the original biblical religion—Judaism—rather than in the derivative religions. Indeed, the Jews could interpret the anti-Jewish attitudes of Christians and Muslims as a manifestation of their anger at having to admit priority of place to the Hebrew Bible. They resented the fact that the Jews were the first to receive divine revelation, and they strove to demonstrate that their religions had come to replace Judaism. One way of doing this was to persecute Jews and denigrate Judaism.

The Bible and rabbinic literature taught Jews that God had chosen the people of Israel for a special mission—to spread monotheism and teach righteousness to the world. This was a difficult and often thankless responsibility; yet this was God's will. The day would come when all the people of the world would recognize the one true God, when the spirit of God would imbue humanity with love, kindness, and righteousness—when the entire world would be blessed with peace. This vision helped Jews transcend the temporary pains they suffered along the way to this goal. They waited patiently for the messiah to redeem them, and to redeem all of humanity.

Why did Jews have to suffer so much? Why were they forced into exile? Why did they have to endure persecution and humiliation at the hands of others? Various answers were suggested by the ancient sacred literature. Jews suffered as punishment for their sins, and the suffering was a means of atonement. Patience in the face of suffering was a great religious virtue, a sign of total faith in God and resignation to God's will. Suffering was an impetus toward repentance and personal spiritual renewal. The *yisurin shel ahavah* (loving chastisements from God) were a means of purification, so that one would be worthy of the blessings of the next world.

Suffering was only a temporary phase that would pass. In this world, it will be replaced by the messianic era. In the next world, it will be replaced by heavenly bliss. Ultimately, the sinners and oppressors will suffer from God's wrath, while the people of Israel and the God of Israel will be vindicated.

The outstanding Jewish sages of medieval Spain had made classic contributions to the study of the Bible and ancient rabbinic literature. They had analyzed Hebrew grammar, composed poetry in the spirit of the Bible and rabbinic teachings, philosophized about the ideas of Judaism, and defended Jewish teachings from the attacks of non-Jewish detractors. Sephardim could point to such luminaries as Yitzhak Alfasi, Shemuel ha-Nagid, Maimonides, Shelomo ibn Gabirol, Yehudah Halevy, Abraham and Moshe ibn Ezra, Nachmanides, Shelomo ben Adret, and so many others. Their contributions to Jewish literature were unsurpassed and were a vital and proud heritage of Sephardic Jewry.

The first generations of Sephardic exiles in the Ottoman Empire not only revered their sages of earlier times, but continued to follow in their footsteps. They, too, devoted themselves to the study of the Bible and rabbinic texts, to Hebrew language and literature.

As an illustration of their intellectual interests, we may consider the list of items published in Istanbul from 1504 to 1593.[1] Of the 228 publications, 40 related to the Bible (i.e., biblical texts, commentaries, sermons); 12 dealt with Hebrew grammar; 45 related to ancient rabbinic literature (i.e., Talmud, Midrash, commentaries); 9 related to poetry. Thus, these topics accounted for a bit more than 42 percent of the entire publication list, an indication of their centrality in the Jewish life of that period.

Among the notable works that emerged among the Sephardic exiles were the biblical commentaries of Rabbi Yitzhak Abravanel (1437–1508), the preeminent Jewish leader and statesman in Spain at the time of the expulsion. Abravanel settled in Naples and then in Venice. His commentaries became classics throughout the Jewish world, including the communities of Sephardim in the Ottoman Empire, and have been reprinted in many editions.

Another classic of the period following the expulsion from Spain was the *Ein Yaacov*, a comprehensive compilation of the aggadic passages of the Talmud, together with commentaries. It was prepared by Rabbi Yaacov ibn Haviv (c. 1450–1516), who had been born in Spain and whose family settled in Salonika, where he served as a rabbi. Several sections were published during his lifetime, and the remainder was published through the efforts of his son Rabbi Levi ibn Haviv (c. 1484–1545), who had left Salonika to settle in Jerusalem, where he became the leading rabbi. The *Ein Yaacov*, first published in full in Salonika in 1516, almost immediately became a standard work throughout the Jewish world and has been reprinted over one hundred times.

In the field of Hebrew poetry, this period also left a lasting impression. The *Lekha Dodi* hymn, composed by Rabbi Shelomo Alkabets (1505–c. 1576) of Salonika and then Safed, has been incorporated into the Friday evening services of Jews throughout the world. Rabbi Eliezer Azikri (1533–1600) of Safed composed the *Yedid Nefesh* hymn, also widely sung on Friday evenings as part of services or around the Sabbath table. Another poet of this period was Rabbi Israel Najara (c. 1555–1628) of Safed, whose most popular hymn is *Y-ah Ribbon Alam*. The poetic productions of these and other Sephardic poets were deeply steeped in biblical and rabbinic literary style and symbolism.

The ongoing commitment to the study of the Bible and rabbinic literature was a basic feature of the intellectual life of the Jews of the Ottoman Empire during the generations after the expulsion from Spain. These classic sources of Jewish teachings enabled them to cope with their crises and to see their lives as part of an eternal divine plan.

Halakhah

Halakhah (Jewish law) is a comprehensive system, governing one's actions from birth to death. The Sabbath, holy days, fast days, and minor holidays maintain a religious rhythm to life. Jewish law is detailed enough to be concerned with how one should tie one's shoes and grand enough to instruct compassionate, generous behavior that will lead to a harmonious society. Halakhah provides a pattern of life that transcends any particular place—the laws and customs of the Sabbath and kashrut may be observed in the same way whether one lived in Spain or in Turkey—or anywhere else in the world. Perhaps more than any other factor, it was Halakhah that enabled Jews to maintain the structure of their lives under varying circumstances. The Sephardic arrivals in the Ottoman Empire, by devoting themselves to Halakhah, could transplant their way of life to their new homes while maintaining familiar and comforting patterns of behavior.

The exiles built their new communities according to the teachings of Halakhah. They quickly developed a communal structure similar to what they had experienced in Spain. They established schools, courts, and their own system of administration and taxation. Since Halakhah dominated Jewish life, rabbis—as halakhic authorities—were highly important leaders and teachers.

The sages of medieval Spain set a firm foundation for the study and codification of Halakhah. The outstanding codifiers of Jewish law—Rabbi Yitzhak Alfasi, Maimonides, and Rabbi Yaacov ben Asher—all had roots in Spain. Rabbeinu Asher, of Ashkenazic origin and training, spent many years as a rabbi in Spain and was surely influenced by Sephardim, just as they were influenced by him. The halakhic methods developed by Sephardic sages were— and continue to be—of monumental significance. Sephardic halakhists generally focused on reaching clear, practical rulings, rather than engaging in legalistic dialectics.

The study of Halakhah among the Sephardic exiles in the Ottoman Empire built on the achievements of the earlier Sephardic rabbis. The classic legal works of Rabbi Yosef Karo (1488–1575), the *Beit Yosef* and the *Shulhan Arukh*, became the foundation stones for the study of Halakhah down to our own day. Sephardic sages achieved a golden age in responsa, an important genre of halakhic literature. Questions on the entire range of law were submitted to the leading rabbis, who then wrote their responses. These responsa were collected and published in volumes, serving as sources of Jewish law for future generations. Among the notable Sephardic responsa writers of the sixteenth century were Rabbis David ibn Abi Zimra, Shemuel de Medina, Yosef Karo, Yaacov Berav, Moshe Alashkar, Yosef Taitatsak, and Levi ibn Haviv. In reviewing the halakhic output of the Sephardic exiles, Professor H. J. Zimmels has noted that it was "amazing that soon after the expulsion in the year 1492 the contributions to the responsa literature by the rabbis who had come from Spain and settled in Turkey reached a height never witnessed before."[2]

In 1504, David and Shemuel Nahmias established the first Hebrew printing press in Istanbul. Their first publication was the code of Jewish law by Rabbi Yaacov ben Asher, the *Arba Turim*. During the period of 1504–1593, a bit over 20 percent (forty-six titles) of the Hebrew publications in Istanbul related to Halakhah (codes, responsa, halakhic commentaries). Many other works of halakhic content were issued by the Hebrew press in Salonika (established in 1515) and other centers of Jewish publication. Clearly, the study and observance of Halakhah were of paramount importance among the Jews of this period.

Kabbalah

Kabbalah, Jewish mysticism, had struck deep roots in medieval Spain. Rabbi Yitzhak the Blind (c. 1160–1235) and his circle of kabbalists made Gerona a major center of Jewish mysticism. Nachmanides (1194–1270), the leading rabbinic figure in Catalonia, spread the teachings of Kabbalah through his profound biblical commentaries. Late in the thirteenth century, Rabbi Moshe de Leon issued the *Zohar*, the classic text of Kabbalah, whose authorship is attributed to the great second-century Talmudic sage Rabbi Shimon bar Yohai.

The Sephardic rabbis of the period of the expulsion from Spain and thereafter drew on the kabbalistic teachings of their predecessors but also made significant contributions of their own. Sephardic yeshivot included Halakhah and Kabbalah as basic elements in their curriculae.[3]

Significantly, the leading halakhists among the Sephardic exiles were also steeped in Kabbalah. Among the most striking examples is Rabbi Yosef Karo, who not only authored the standard code of Jewish law but also wrote *Maggid Mesharim*, a book recording revelations he received from an angel who visited him regularly. Professor Zwi Werblowsky pointed out that Rabbi Karo was able to compartmentalize the two disciplines of Halakhah and Kabbalah so that "his charismatic or mystical life did not spill over into his daylight activities. The Karo of the codes and the responsa remained healthy, realistic, and down to earth."[4]

Halakhah and Kabbalah were viewed not as two opposing disciplines, but as partners in the formation of a unified spiritual worldview. Legalism and mysticism were interrelated and interdependent; at root, both systems were seeking to hear the word of God and come closer to the divine.

During the sixteenth century, Kabbalah blossomed throughout the Sephardic diaspora of the Ottoman Empire. Its most spectacular flowering was in Safed. This city in the north of the Land of Israel attracted a remarkable group of sages—including such figures as Rabbis Yosef Karo, Shelomo Alkabets, Moshe Cordovero, Eliyahu de Vidas, Moshe Alsheikh, and David ibn Abi Zimra—whose influence has been felt throughout the ensuing generations to our own day.

Safed was home to Rabbi Yitzhak Luria (1534–72), known as the *Ari ha-Kadosh* (the Holy Ari). His teachings became the foundation of kabbalistic study for his generation and generations to come. Although he wrote very little, his ideas were published and popularized by his devoted students, particularly Rabbi Hayyim Vital. The Ari developed a kabbalistic system that viewed the universe as a battleground between the power of holiness and the power of evil. It was the special responsibility of the people of Israel to redeem the sparks of holiness, overcome evil, and return the universe to its pristine wholeness. By fulfilling the commandments of the Torah with the proper kabbalistic devotion and intent, Jews were thereby engaged in *tikkun*, repairing and restoring the spiritual cosmos.

Professor Joseph Dan has suggested that according to the Ari, history "is the story of the repeated attempts of the good divine powers to rescue the sparks and to bring unity to the earthly and divine worlds. Previous attempts had always failed."[5] Rabbi Luria and his disciples believed that messianic redemption was nearing, when evil would be overcome once and for all. The Ari taught that God, in creating the world, had gone into a sort of self-inflicted exile. God, too, was awaiting the time of ultimate redemption when the power of holiness would be entirely victorious.

The framework of exile and redemption inherent in Lurianic Kabbalah was relevant to the spiritual situation of the post-expulsion Sephardic communities. They could view their own exile as a reflection and symbol of God's exile. If they did their share in redeeming the sparks of holiness, they could play a role in ultimate redemption. In this way, they could find meaning in their suffering and work constructively toward a better world.[6]

Kabbalah depicted events in this world as being symbolic of spiritual happenings in higher spheres of existence. Human deeds affected the mysterious spiritual world beyond. The struggle against injustice in this world was symbolic of the battle of holiness against "the other side," the power of evil. The fulfillment of a mitzvah was a cosmic act that influenced the spiritual well-being of the universe, while the commission of a sin shook the metaphysical foundations of existence. Rabbi Moshe Cordovero (1522–70) expressed a basic kabbalistic idea when he taught that "just as a man conducts himself here below, so will he be worthy of opening that higher quality from above. As he behaves, so will be the affluence from above and he will cause that quality to shine upon earth."[7]

Kabbalistic teachings spread widely throughout the Sephardic diaspora. Whereas the Jews in Spain were more apt to engage in philosophic study than in Kabbalah, the exiles and subsequent generations increasingly turned away from philosophy. Kabbalah responded more directly to their spiritual needs and offered a host of specific practices and meditations that could be implemented by all pious people—not just an intellectual elite.

The increasing role of Kabbalah in the religious life of Sephardim contributed toward a greater desire for piety and saintliness. The Ari's demand for Jews to engage in *tikkun* underscored the cosmic meaning of each righteous deed. Even the performance of a simple mitzvah might merit the arrival of messianic redemption. The all-consuming responsibility of *tikkun* gave meaning and direction to life, enabling people to transcend their problems by focusing on higher spiritual matters.

According to Professor Joseph Dan, "ethics in Lurianic kabbala is no longer an attempt to achieve personal perfection. It is a set of instructions directing the individual how to participate in the common struggle of the Jewish people."[8] This Lurianic teaching was foreshadowed by the view of Rabbi Moshe Cordovero, who wrote:

> All Israel are related one to the other, for their souls are united, and in each soul there is a portion of all the others.... When one Israelite sins, he wrongs not only his own soul but the portion which all the others possess in him.[9]

Mystical pietists stressed ethical behavior and the scrupulous observance of the rituals of Judaism. They met regularly in small groups to evaluate their lives, to criticize each others' sins, and to encourage each other to ever higher levels of spiritual perfection. Kabbalists, such as Rabbis Moshe Cordovero, Abraham Galante, and Abraham Halevy, compiled lists of practices for the benefit of their disciples.[10] The mystical/ethical/ritual practices of the Ari were carefully noted by his students and were widely publicized and emulated. Sages of sixteenth-century Safed produced outstanding works of kabbalistic ethics, such as *Reshit Hokhma* by Rabbi Eliyahu de Vidas and *Sefer Hareidim* by Rabbi Eliezer Azikri.

Mystical ethics was a fusion of Halakhah and Kabbalah. Halakhah was deepened by its mystical interpretations and applications. Kabbalah was tied to the sphere of everyday life by the dictates of Halakhah. These two spiritual disciplines merged not merely in the elite sages, but among the masses of Sephardim. If Halakhah provided a pattern and structure for their daily lives, Kabbalah provided meaning and hope.

Philosophy and General Wisdom

Medieval Sephardic Jews produced significant philosophic works and made important contributions to the sciences and mathematics. They were distinguished for their ability to blend religious traditionalism with active participation in the general intellectual life of their time. Maimonides (1135–1204) was the paradigm of a sage who was not only a master of Halakhah, but also a world-class philosopher and medical doctor.

Maimonides represented the rationalistic, philosophic tradition of Sephardic Jewry. He set forth the basic principles of faith, interpreted the Bible in consonance with these principles (e.g., allegorizing the anthropomorphic and anthropopathic references to God), and insisted on a rational understanding of biblical and rabbinic passages. He scorned those fundamentalists who accepted all the words of the ancient rabbinic sages literally, without seeking to understand their deeper meanings.

> One must feel sorry for their foolishness. According to their understanding, they are honoring and elevating our sages, when in fact they are lowering them to the end of lowliness; and they do not even realize this. By heaven! This group is dissipating the glory of Torah and clouding its lights, and they place the Torah of God against its own intention.[11]

According to Maimonides' approach, one must evaluate and interpret rabbinic statements that seemed unreasonable. The rabbis were, after all, wise and reasonable people; their words would necessarily conform to reason. If their statements seemed irrational, one needed to recognize that they often spoke in allegorical and symbolic—rather than literal—language.

Rabbi Abraham, son of Maimonides, argued that the search for truth depends on reason.

> We, and every intelligent and wise person, are obligated to evaluate each idea and each statement, to find the way in which to understand it; to prove the proof and establish that which is worthy of being established, and to annul that which is worthy of being annulled.... We see that our sages themselves said: if it is a Halakhah [universally accepted legal tradition] we will accept it; but if it is a ruling [based on individual opinion], there is room for discussion.[12]

The rationalist tradition was maintained among the first generations of Sephardic exiles to the Ottoman Empire. Rabbi Abraham ibn Migash, for example, argued eloquently on behalf of a rationalistic approach: "One must know that the ultimate human achievement is attained in the most honorable human power—the power of reason."[13] No one can learn all the branches of wisdom (e.g., medicine, science) simply by studying the Torah. Rather, each field of knowledge needs to be studied from its own experts. Ibn Migash was critical of those who dabbled in Kabbalah, rather than seeking truth through philosophical quest. He himself eschewed kabbalistic study, devoting himself instead to rationalistic pursuits.[14]

A number of Sephardic intellectuals engaged in philosophical study and discussion. Among them were Rabbi Yosef Taitatsak, Rabbi Yitzhak Aderbi, and Rabbi Shelomo le-Bet ha-Levi, all of Salonika.[15] Yehudah Zarco, a Hebrew poet who lived in Rhodes and then moved to another community in the Ottoman Empire, wrote a poetic/philosophic work entitled *Lehem Yehudah*, in which he described his participation in a circle of young Jews who discussed literature and philosophy. The upshot of his work was to extol reason and call for the control of one's emotions.[16]

Yet, in spite of manifestations of philosophical endeavors, the ascendant attitude among the Sephardic exiles veered away from

philosophy and toward Kabbalah. Indeed, Rabbi Yosef Yaavets, a
leading rabbi among the Jews expelled from Spain, blamed philosophy for the breakdown of religious faith among Spanish Jews. Had
they clung to the pure study of Torah, they would have fared much
better. Philosophy had confused them, and led many of them to
apostasy. Rabbi Yaavets castigated those who left the study of Talmud
in favor of pursuing philosophy. As a general rule, "one should not
learn from their books [philosophy] and not listen to their sages—
even when they say the truth, one should not listen to them."[17]

Rabbi Meir ben Gabbai, a Sephardic exile who apparently
found haven in Turkey, also argued against philosophical study.
Philosophy could not be trusted as a source of truth, since philosophers of one generation were refuted by philosophers of the next
generations. The Jewish people had a source of immutable truth,
the Torah, and had no need of the ephemeral wisdom provided by
philosophy.

> There is no wisdom and no understanding except in the
> study of Torah and in the keeping of its commandments.
> Those who keep the Torah call out to God and He answers
> them. This is their wisdom and their understanding in the
> eyes of the nations—not the inquiry into the various
> branches of philosophy.... Philosophy is forbidden to any-
> one who would call himself a Jew.[18]

The viewpoint of rabbis Yaavets and Gabbai reflected the
growing normative attitude among the Sephardim in the Ottoman
Empire. While there was still evidence of serious philosophic activity during the sixteenth century, this faded away by the seventeenth
century. The Jewish community turned inward intellectually. It was
separated by language and culture from the dominant surrounding
society; it was separated from the intellectual ferment in Spain and
the rest of Europe. It sought truth and solace from within the con-
fines of the inward-looking aspects of its own spiritual traditions.

5

Turning Points

The tiny Jewish minority of the Ottoman Empire flourished fairly well during the sixteenth century. Although Jews were subjected to various legal disabilities and humiliations, they rose to prominence in commerce, medicine, and other fields of endeavor. Individual Jews enjoyed the confidence of the sultans and even served as respected advisers.

The Spanish Jews brought needed skills to the expanding Ottoman Empire. While transforming the Jewish communities of Turkey and the Balkans into islands of Judeo-Spanish civilization, the Sephardim played a role in the larger society as well. They were able to compete successfully not only with the Muslim population, but also with the Greek and Armenian Christian minorities.

As long as the Ottoman Empire was strong and confident, the position of its non-Muslim minorities was relatively good. Muslim rulers focused on the empire's power and prosperity and were pleased to have the active participation of Jews and Christians in advancing the empire's fortunes. However, when general conditions deteriorated, the minorities' situation worsened accordingly.

Standstill and Decline

Professor Avigdor Levy has noted that the Ottoman social and political fabric began to show signs of fatigue during the last decades of the sixteenth century. The empire entered a period of stagnation and decline.[1] While there were periods of stability and recovery, the Ottoman Empire from 1580 to 1826 was in a state of disintegration.

By 1584, a serious economic crisis led to a substantial devaluation of the empire's currency. The debasement of currency was accompanied by rampant inflation. This crisis was to last through the middle of the seventeenth century and had a negative impact on the economic health of the empire.

During this period, the Ottoman Empire suffered a general and prolonged stagnation in trade. Since many of the empire's merchants were Christians and Jews, these groups were particularly hurt by the decline in international commerce.

The economic decline of the empire was exacerbated by the tremendous advances among European competitors. European nations were sending explorers and establishing colonies in the New World; the Atlantic Ocean grew in commercial importance while the Mediterranean Sea saw its status decline. Likewise, the Europeans were introducing new technological means of production, notably in the manufacture of textiles. The textile industry of Turkey—in which many Jews were engaged—suffered dramatically from European competition.

The marked decline in Ottoman international trade adversely affected Jews who were involved in exporting and importing. Although some were able to maintain a significant role in international commerce, the overall Jewish economic position in this area was sharply curtailed. Jews were forced out from positions as principals in large-scale trade to secondary occupations as agents, brokers, and interpreters. This resulted in a considerable diminution of the wealthiest Jewish group.[2]

Jews also lost ground in the area of tax farming. They were gradually reduced to secondary positions as agents or managers of tax farms, with most of the profits now going to government officials and soldiers.[3]

While a number of Jewish doctors continued to serve sultans and other high officials, fewer Jews were becoming doctors. As of the mid-seventeenth century, the number of Jews in the medical profession had decreased markedly. This was symptomatic of Jewish decline in so many other areas.[4]

By the mid-seventeenth century, then, the economic situation of the Jews of Turkey had undergone erosion. Their wealthiest group was smaller and less prosperous. As their business enterprises shrank, their ability to hire fellow Jews as employees also was curtailed. Thus, unemployment and underemployment became more widespread within the Jewish community.

The influence of wealthy Jews as spokesmen to the government had also diminished. This, in turn, weakened the political position of Jews and gave them less access to the seats of power of the empire.

Since the wealthy Jews were the ones who provided the most significant support for Jewish institutions—including schools and publishing houses—the decline in their number and level of wealth adversely affected intellectual life among the community at large. The economic stagnation and decline were accompanied by cultural stagnation and decline.

Along with the economic woes, residents of the Ottoman Empire were negatively affected by wars. Ottoman military ventures, increasingly ending in humiliation, were expensive and required heavy taxation. Moreover, wars in the frontier provinces led to internal unrest and rebellions. Jews, along with other Ottoman residents, were vulnerable to predation and attack, and Jews seem to have been among the first victims of the prevailing disorder.[5] The Ottomans remained an imperial power until late in the seventeenth century, when they failed in their second siege of

Vienna in 1683. After that retreat, it was clear that the balance of power had shifted against them. Ottoman military might declined, reaching a low point at the end of the eighteenth century and the early decades of the nineteenth century.[6]

The deterioration in the economic and military spheres was reflected in the general breakdown of Ottoman government. Dr. Bernard Lewis observed that the decline could be seen in the Turkish archives. In the sixteenth century, the archives were kept with meticulous, conscientious, and efficient management. In the seventeenth century, there was growing neglect. By the eighteenth century, the system of archives had collapsed.[7]

Messianic Longings

In witnessing their worsening situation, the Jews of the Ottoman Empire must have felt increasingly powerless. Many of their problems stemmed from political, economic, and military decisions over which they had no control. They were simply pawns in a larger game of international power struggles—and their side was losing.

As if their own problems were not troubling enough, they also were aware of tragedies that were befalling Jewish communities in other lands. During the sixteenth and early seventeenth centuries, conversos from Spain and Portugal were arriving in the Ottoman Empire and returning to Judaism. They told of the brutalities of the Inquisition and of the ongoing sufferings of those of Jewish ancestry living in the Iberian Peninsula.

Jews in Europe were subjected to various humiliations and persecutions. Jewish ghettos were established in such cities as Venice, Ferrara, Padua, and Vienna. In 1648–49 and thereafter, the Cossacks killed thousands of Jews in the Ukraine and southeast Poland in a series of concerted pogroms. Anti-Jewish riots broke out in Lemberg and Cracow in 1664.

In the face of so much distress, the Jews of the Ottoman Empire—and Jews everywhere—wondered how their situation could be ameliorated. Their answer was: divine intervention. They waited for the Almighty to send the messiah to redeem them from their suffering.

Indeed, messianic longings had simmered among the Jewish people since the time of the destruction of the Second Temple in Jerusalem by the Romans in 70 CE. Jews prayed for the time when they would be restored to their homeland in Israel, when they would be free from the yoke of foreign domination, when their enemies would cease to oppress them. The coming of the messiah would usher in an era of peace and prosperity and bring an end to Jewish suffering.

Messianic expectations were raised during the period of the expulsion of Jews from Spain. Rabbi Yitzhak Abravanel wrote three books in which he explained that the sufferings of the Spanish exiles signaled the onset of the messianic era. He predicted that the messiah would come in the year 1503.[8]

Rabbi Yosef Shaltiel, writing in Rhodes in 1495, expressed a similar belief that the arrival of the messiah was imminent: "I think that the sufferings which the Jews have found in all the kingdoms of Edom [Christendom] from 5250–5255 [1490–1495] constitute a period of sorrow for Jacob from which he will be saved; these are the pains which will usher in the Messiah."[9] Others echoed these sentiments: redemption was near.[10]

But the messiah did not come in 1503 or in the subsequent years. Jews continued to wait and hope. By the mid-seventeenth century, they thought their prayers were finally to be answered.[11]

Sabbatai Sevi

Jewish messianic hopes came to center on an enigmatic and charismatic figure named Sabbatai Sevi. Born on the fast of the ninth of Av 5386 (1626) in Izmir, he was to become the most notorious figure within the Judeo-Spanish-speaking world and a major personality in Jewish history.

At around age fifteen, Sabbatai Sevi began to immerse himself in the study of Kabbalah. He turned to a life of asceticism and solitude. By his early twenties, he had experienced unusual states of exaltation, but also was plagued by periods of dejection and profound melancholy. He was to manifest these bipolar traits for the rest of his life. At times, he experienced "illumination," and at times he suffered from the "hiding of God's face."

Sabbatai Sevi introduced shocking elements into his religious observances. He pronounced God's ineffable name in public, although that name was only to be pronounced by the high priest on Yom Kippur while officiating in the Holy of Holies at the Temple in Jerusalem. Sabbatai transgressed other laws and traditions of Judaism, going so far as to recite a special blessing over these transgressions. His bizarre behavior led to his being excommunicated several times by the rabbis of Izmir.

On his travels, he attracted followers who were much impressed with his spiritual personality. He arrived in Jerusalem in the summer of 1662 and remained there for a year. Among his pious practices, he fasted throughout the week, taking meals only on the Sabbath. He sought solitude, periodically spending several days in the mountains and caves of the Judean hills. He claimed to hear voices from graves. His admirers reported that when Sabbatai recited psalms, his face became intense and radiant so that looking at him was like looking at a fire.

A young man steeped in Kabbalah, Nathan of Gaza, claimed to receive a prophetic vision that Sabbatai Sevi was the messiah. Nathan conveyed this prophecy to Sabbatai, who then (May 31, 1665) proclaimed himself to be the messiah. Nathan worked energetically to gain adherents for the incipient messianic movement. The majority of the Jews in Gaza and Hebron, and many in Safed, became believers in Sabbatai's claim. Most of the rabbinic leaders in Jerusalem, though, were strongly opposed to this movement, and they excommunicated Sabbatai.

The would-be messiah left Jerusalem in the summer of 1665 and went to Aleppo, where he was well received. In September he returned to his home town of Izmir. While the messianic movement had opponents, it grew spectacularly not only among the masses of Jews, but even among the rabbinic leaders. Messianic frenzy spread throughout the Jewish world, far beyond the boundaries of the Ottoman Empire.

Sabbatai Sevi abolished the fasts of the seventeenth of Tammuz and the ninth of Av, telling the people to celebrate these days as festivals. In messianic times, these days of mourning were to be transformed into days of joy—and messianic times had arrived!

Sabbatai Sevi was expected to redeem the Jewish people from exile in the spring of 1666. In anticipation of this event, many Jews devoted themselves to greater piety so that they would be worthy to merit the expected redemption. They paid little attention to practical matters; after all, if messianic redemption was imminent, there was no point in making long-term business plans or investments.

The believers in Sabbatai Sevi became dominant in Jewish communities throughout the Ottoman Empire—and throughout the world. Opponents were ridiculed and even threatened with bodily harm. In September 1665, twenty-five rabbis in Istanbul issued a writ of excommunication against Sabbatai Sevi. These rabbis and other opponents of the messianic movement urged the Jewish community to be reasonable. They feared that the messianic enthusiasm would lead to disappointment and disaster. But the words of the opponents had little effect on the messianic enthusiasts.

In the winter of 1665, while in Izmir, Sabbatai Sevi again pronounced God's ineffable name. He ate forbidden fat and encouraged his followers to commit certain sins. Rabbi Hayyim Benveniste, the outstanding rabbi of Izmir at the time, had initially been opposed to the messianic movement, but he was unable to stem its popularity and seems ultimately to have joined the movement himself.

In February 1666, Sabbatai Sevi went to Istanbul. His adherents believed that the stage was set for the messiah to come before the sultan and for the sultan to give his turban to Sabbatai in acknowledgment of the Jewish Messiah's power.

The months of messianic agitation among the Jews did not go unnoticed by the Ottoman officials. They were disturbed by the cessation of normal business life among Jews. Would their belief in Sabbatai Sevi's claims lead to an actual rebellion against Ottoman rule?

The sultan had Sabbatai arrested and imprisoned. After two months, Sabbatai was transferred to a prison in Gallipoli. Yet, Sabbatai's followers were not at all discouraged by this course of events. Rabbi Ya'akov Sasportas, an opponent of Sabbateanism, noted that "although he [Sabbatai Sevi] was imprisoned in Gallipoli, nevertheless this was not sufficient to weaken the strength of his believers; on the contrary, they bolstered him with false and farfetched attributes, testifying that he performed a number of miracles and wonders."[12] Sabbatai's adherents came in large numbers to Gallipoli to pay homage to their master.

In September, Sabbatai was transferred to Edirne. The sultan gave him the choice of converting to Islam or being executed. To the astonishment of the Jews, Sabbatai chose apostasy, changing his name to Mehemed Effendi. The sultan, pleased with this decision, treated the new convert with honor, believing that Sabbatai would influence his adherents to follow his example. Indeed, Sabbatai's wife and a number of devotees converted to Islam. These apostates believed that Sabbatai's conversion to Islam was only a temporary measure, a necessary step on the path to messianic redemption. He first had to enter into the depths of sin and impurity and then would emerge in all his splendor and power. They demonstrated their absolute faith in him by following him into Islam.

While a minority of Sabbatai's adherents tried to justify his apostasy, the majority realized that this action totally undermined Sabbatai's claim to be the messiah. It was impossible that the Jewish messiah should commit the heinous sin of adopting another religion. The Jews had been misled and betrayed by Sabbatai. The problem now was: how could they resume their lives in an unredeemed world? The masses of Jews had invested so much hope in Sabbatai Sevi and had neglected worldly matters for so many months: how were they to recover from the bursting of the messianic bubble? Instead of being liberated from the yoke of foreign domination, they were now subjected to ridicule from their Muslim and Christian neighbors.

A period of spiritual turmoil ensued. Followers of Sabbatai Sevi, including Nathan of Gaza, continued to rally Jews to have faith in the apostate messiah. In 1667, Sabbatai Sevi's wife bore him a son, whom he circumcised according to Jewish practice. Sabbatai was also known to worship in synagogues and to follow some Jewish religious practices. These actions spurred the faithful in their belief that he remained a Jew in his heart and would one day return openly to Judaism and assume his role as messiah. When Sabbatai Sevi died on Yom Kippur in 1676, his followers strove to keep this news secret. A notion spread that Sabbatai had not really died at all, but had been removed to paradise, where he would remain until the day of redemption. A group of believers, known as Donmeh, continued for centuries to maintain faith in Sabbatai's second coming. Amazingly, Sabbateanism survived long after Sabbatai's death. The deep faith in his role as messiah could not be easily brushed aside or forgotten.

After Sabbatai Sevi

Following the conversion of Sabbatai Sevi, the rabbinic establishment had the difficult task of ministering to the spiritual needs of their discouraged communities. The despair and frustration were palpable. The rabbis of Istanbul proclaimed a punishment of excommunication for anyone who continued to believe in the messianic claim of Sabbatai Sevi and who observed practices associated with his movement. In the summer of 1667, the rabbis of Istanbul and Izmir made a point of stressing the importance of fasting on the ninth of Av, a fast day that had been abolished by Sabbatai Sevi.

Writing in Venice, Rabbi Shemuel Aboab noted that rabbis sought to destroy all memory of Sabbatai Sevi. They burned records and papers that contained his name, and they refused to mention him. Rabbis hoped that by blotting out Sabbatai Sevi's name, people would go on with their lives and forget about the pseudo-messiah. But the aftermath of Sabbateanism was to leave deep scars in the lives and memories of the Jewish people.[13]

In Jewish communities of western Europe, a reaction to the Sabbatean debacle was to downplay the study of Kabbalah. It was believed that the Jews had been susceptible to the messianic frenzy because they had been too strongly influenced by kabbalistic teachings. It was time to return to a more rational view of Judaism and to be more practical in dealing with the challenges of life. In Amsterdam, for example, the Portuguese congregation removed kabbalistic references from the prayer books and eliminated kabbalistic practices.

The turn away from Kabbalah reflected a new mindset among western Jews. They grew increasingly impatient with dreams of messianic redemption and felt the need to engage in practical measures to improve their own situation. The winds of enlightenment and emancipation began to stir them. Professor Yitzhak Baer wrote: "In Sephardic circles of the period, we find for the first time an optimistic consciousness of progress.... From the Sephardim of England and Holland, rationalism spread to the Jewish skeptics in France and even to the Jews of Germany."[14] Western Jews began to feel the desire to "modernize," to adapt to conditions in the lands in which they lived, and to become active participants in their societies.

Rabbi Moshe Hagiz (c. 1672–1751), a relentless opponent of Sabbateanism, was disappointed to find that affluent Jews in Amsterdam had grown quite comfortable living in Dutch society. They said mockingly, "If the messiah is going to come to equalize the poor and the rich, let him not come; what do we need him for?"[15] Others said they would be glad to welcome the messiah, since he would then relieve them of the responsibility of taking care of the poor! Western Jewry was inuring itself from the impact of any future messianic pretenders; they had learned their lesson from Sabbatai Sevi's failure, and they were not going to fall into the same trap a second time.

While western Jewry moved in the direction of rationalism and practicality, eastern Jewry moved even further in the direction of Kabbalah and otherworldliness. Professor Jacob Barnai noted:

> Sabbateanism and its failure strongly encouraged the study of mysticism in the Ottoman Empire, rather than restraining it as occurred in Western Europe and, to a lesser extent, in Eastern Europe. The principal trends of the spiritual works of the sages of the empire were in the direction of mysticism rather than rationalism.[16]

We will discuss the post-Sabbatean spiritual life of Ottoman Jewry in the next chapter.

Solomon Rosanes (1862–1938), a Bulgarian-born Sephardic historian with strong Haskalah (Enlightenment) leanings, lamented the precipitous decline of Ottoman Jewry in the wake of the Sabbatai Sevi episode:

> Then all the glory was taken away from Turkish Jewry, never to return, and then the end came for the high ethical and material standing of the Jews in the capitol and the other cities.... On all sides there was retrogression and a change for the worse in the social and political life of the Jews.... All these scenes were caused by the false messiah Sabbatai Sevi and his band of prophets. They did not succeed in bringing the leaders of the generation to their senses, to see that the time had come finally to bring an end to the messianic delusion and Kabbalah, and to destroy the source within the Jewish people from which all the fantasizing ones drew their inspiration, i.e., the *Zohar* and the Kabbalah.[17]

While Rosanes's anti-Kabbalah bias is obvious enough, nevertheless he touched upon an important historical fact. The life of the Jews of the Ottoman Empire clearly underwent a change for the worse in the years following Sabbatai Sevi's failed movement.

Although signs of decline in the Jewish condition were evident even before Sabbatai, the situation afterward deteriorated dramatically. Surely, the woes of Ottoman Jewry were exacerbated by economic and political causes; yet, the trauma of Sabbateanism was a major component in the decline of Ottoman Jewry. The Jews of Turkey seem to have been more directly impacted by Sabbatai's downfall than were other communities. After all, Sabbatai was one of them, a child of Izmir, a student of their teachers, a product of their Judeo-Spanish civilization.

Decline

The decline of Ottoman Jewry did not happen in one plunge, nor was it a process that affected all communities at the same pace. Istanbul and Salonika continued to be important centers of Jewish scholarship and maintained active publishing houses. The community in Izmir seems to have been doing well until a disastrous earthquake in 1688 caused immense damage and loss of life. It took many years for the community to reconstitute itself following the earthquake.

Some observers thought the Jews of Turkey were doing well for themselves. Michel Febvre, a Capuchin monk who spent eighteen years living in the Orient and published his observations in 1682, described the Jews of Turkey as being adroit and industrious. Their services were needed by everyone. Jews had a unique ability to evaluate merchandise, and they knew which places sold which types of merchandise and at what prices. In their business acumen, they surpassed the Greeks and Armenians.[18]

In 1717, Lady Mary Wortley Montagu, wife of the British ambassador in Istanbul, had the impression that Jews dominated the city's economy:

> I observed most of the rich tradesmen were Jews. That peo-
> ple are an incredible power in this country. They have many
> privileges … and have formed a very considerable com-

monwealth here, being judged by their own laws, and have drawn the whole trade of the empire into their hands.... No bargain is made, no bribe received, no merchandise disposed of, but what passes through their hands. They are the physicians, the stewards, and interpreters of the great men.[19]

In spite of these observations—which seem to be exaggeratedly optimistic about the Jews' economic successes—the overall trend during the eighteenth century was negative. The pace of Ottoman disintegration seems to have accelerated after the disastrous Ottoman wars with Russia in 1768–74 and with a Russian-Austrian coalition in 1787–92. Jews, along with other residents of the empire, were required to pay very high taxes to finance the war effort. Jews were also among those impressed into the military. Reflective of the economic distress of this period, the annual budget of the Jewish community in Istanbul in 1771–72 showed a serious deficit. The community's debts were more than six and one half times greater than its annual income. Servicing the debt amounted to nearly 45 percent of the total income. Over 75 percent of the budget was earmarked for various government taxes and for servicing the community's debt, with less than 25 percent being devoted to the actual expenses of operating the community.[20]

If the major Jewish community of Istanbul was suffering from the economic decline, this was also true for the many smaller communities throughout the empire. The situation in Rhodes is a case in point. During the tenure of Rabbi Ezra Malki as chief rabbi (from 1726 until his death in 1768), poverty had become widespread among the Jews of Rhodes. The community could hardly care for its own poor, let alone help poor Jews who came to their town. A letter to Rabbi Malki described the situation in striking terms: "The screaming has increased in the markets and in the streets, and anyone who hears the words of the visiting poor and the curses which they curse and the screams which they scream— the hair on his head will stand on end."[21]

A description of conditions during the early nineteenth century was no better: "Poverty has increased in our city and the Jews have become very poor. They scream for food and livelihood and they are not answered."[22] The community's chief rabbi, Michael Yaacov Israel, in 1849 noted that his community had borrowed a considerable sum of money from a Jew of Tiberias. When a collector arrived to receive payment for the loan, he found that the community treasury lacked the funds to repay its debt. Rabbi Israel himself had to guarantee that the debt would be repaid within a year and a half.[23] A mid-century occupational profile of the Jews of Rhodes was provided by Rabbi Raphael Yitzhak Israel, who traveled through Europe to raise funds for the community of Rhodes, since many Jewish homes and buildings had been severely damaged by earthquakes and fires. Rabbi Israel reported that half of Rhodes's three hundred Jewish families were extremely poor. Sixty Jews worked as messengers or porters. There were ten shoemakers, six tailors, three barbers, and a perfume maker. Several Jews were employed as translators for foreign consulates in Rhodes. The rabbi also noted that there were some wealthy Jewish businessmen, albeit a small number.[24] Indeed, Bohor Alhadeff established a banking house in Rhodes in 1819. Later known as Salomon Alhadeff's Sons, this bank grew into one of the powerful financial institutions of the Levant. Other Jews in Rhodes also engaged in banking, investments, and trade. Thus, although the large majority of the Jewish community had fallen into poverty, there was still an elite Jewish business class. This was true not only in Rhodes, but in the Ottoman Empire as a whole.

The first decades of the nineteenth century witnessed the lowest point of the Jewish conditions in the Ottoman Empire. The general impoverishment that had set in during the eighteenth century grew more severe during the early nineteenth century. Moreover,

> the many wars of this period, the uprisings, rebellions and general disorder, all exposed the Jewish community, one of

the smallest and weakest groups in the empire, to attack, plunder, and oppression. From practically every corner of the Empire, reports of massacres, murders, and pillage of Jews have survived.[25]

Greek Jewry suffered tremendous losses during the Greek War of Independence (1821–30). In 1834, Jews in the Land of Israel were attacked and murdered in the course of peasant uprisings.

The deep gloom of Ottoman Jewry reached its nadir in 1826 when the three wealthiest and most prominent leaders of the Istanbul Jewish community—Yeshaya Adjiman, Chelibi Bohor Carmona, and Yehezkel Gabbai—were executed and their property expropriated. Their downfall was linked to the suppression of the Janissary Corps, with which they had financial dealings. The Jews understood the event for what it was: the murder and plunder of their three outstanding leaders. The entire Jewish community attended the funerals and mourning ceremonies, and the memory of this disaster lingered on for many years.[26]

As the political and economic position of the Jews sank, so was there a serious decline in cultural and intellectual life. Children from poor homes had to forgo advanced education in order to find jobs to help with the family's finances. Opportunities for real economic advancement were few. Workers put in long hours to earn meager livings. They had neither the strength nor the time to engage in serious study. The knowledge of the Hebrew language declined, so that most Jewish men could read their prayers in Hebrew with little or no comprehension. Formal education for girls or women continued to be virtually nonexistent and did not start to gain importance until the latter half of the nineteenth century. In the midst of this darkness, what provided light in the Jewish dwelling places? What were the sources of their spiritual consolation?

6

Midrashic/Kabbalistic Judaism

A nineteenth-century writer, A. Ubicini, offered his impressions of Turkish Jewry. He noted that little by little "the taste for study and letters was lost among the Jews of Turkey." Jews were struck

> with a kind of apathy, and they saw themselves gradually dis-possessed of their positions as interpreters and other lucra-tive functions which they had occupied at the Sublime Porte [the Sultan's court] and in the chanceries. Later even the humbler jobs which they had retained, whether in the customs or finances of the Empire or in the households of the pashas, were taken from them by the Armenians.

The Jews watched "with apparent indifference" as their riches passed into the hands of their economic rivals.

Ubicini was perceptive enough to look beyond these negative evaluations of the Jews. If Jews had degenerated and had allowed themselves to fall

> to the lowest rank of the nations subject to the Porte, they compensate for this inferiority by economic and moral virtues which place them well above the Christians. No

community is as well administered as theirs. One rarely hears that a Jew had apostasized. Their morals are strict, never any scandal among them.... The disorders and scandals so common among the Greeks and Armenians, simony, extortion, drunkenness, fraud, theft and murder are unknown among the Jews.[1]

An English visitor to Istanbul in 1828 described the Jews of the city as a degraded and despised group. "Throughout the Ottoman dominions, their pusillanimity is so excessive, that they will flee before the uplifted hand of a child."[2] In 1836, another observer thought the Jews of Istanbul had "a subdued and spiritless expression." They were subjected to contemptuous hatred by the Muslims, and even Muslim children would insult Jews without fear of reprisal.[3]

What had happened to these proud Sephardic Jews whose forbears had brought the culture and traditions of Spanish Jewry to the Ottoman Empire? How had this confident, capable, and energetic people fallen into a seeming torpor, so that they appeared to others to be apathetic and subdued? How did they understand their own condition?

Spiritual Restructuring

With the collapse of Sabbatai Sevi's messianic movement, something snapped within the spiritual life of Ottoman Jewry. They had invested so much hope in imminent redemption, they were dazed when this hope was dashed. How were they to pick up the pieces of their disrupted lives? They had believed with all their hearts and souls that Sabbatai Sevi was going to save the Jewish people, restore them to their Promised Land, enable them to live happy and peaceful lives, take revenge on their enemies. Giving up their faith in Sabbatai's mission was difficult and painful, almost too much to bear. From the verge of salvation, the Jews were plunged to the depths of despair.

The religious leadership of Ottoman Jewry had choices to make as to how to guide their communities. They could have called for a turn away from Kabbalah and in favor of a renewed emphasis on rationalism and philosophy. They could have encouraged this-worldly practicality by urging the Jews to learn Turkish and other European languages so as to be better able to compete in the marketplace. They could have promoted an activist view of life, where Jews would see themselves as responsible for their own destiny and would energize themselves to meet the challenges that faced them. But, for the most part, the religious leadership of the post-Sabbatai era did not make these choices.

The rabbis chose to draw on the religious traditions that had the strongest "folk" elements. The midrashic literature going back to Talmudic times was, in fact, largely directed toward the interests and intellectual capacities of the masses. The Midrash was filled with stories, parables, miracles, and wonders. In the world of Midrash, pious people were visited by Elijah the prophet, spoke with angels, and were rewarded for their good deeds and punished for their sins.

Maimonides had pointed out that the Rabbis of the Midrash often used symbolic language to convey moral lessons and that their words were not to be taken literally. Indeed, as noted earlier, he insisted that the Rabbis of the Midrash were men of reason, whose "unreasonable" words must be understood as allegorical or hyperbolical. The philosophical and literary approach of Maimonides, though, held little sway among those who eschewed philosophy and embraced Kabbalah. For them, the words of the ancient Rabbis were sacred and literally true.

Midrashic Judaism (i.e., that which takes the Midrash/Aggadah literally rather than allegorically) was propounded by leading Sephardic sages of the generation of the expulsion from Spain. Rabbi Yosef Yaavets stated that if one came across a rabbinic passage that seemed odd, "he should suspect his own intelligence, not the intelligence of our sages and their words, which were spoken in truth."[4] Rabbi David ibn Abi Zimra taught that the Aggadah was true and essential, given from Heaven like the rest of the Oral Torah. And just as the Oral Torah is interpreted with thirteen principles, so the Aggadah is interpreted with thirty-six principles. "And these principles were transmitted to Moses our teacher at Sinai."[5]

In the generation after Sabbatai Sevi, Rabbi Moshe Hagiz (c. 1672–1751) was an important religious figure who represented the general trend to bolster rabbinic authority. A tireless opponent of Sabbateanism, Rabbi Hagiz was born and raised in Jerusalem. In 1694, he left the Holy Land and traveled through the Jewish communities of the diaspora to raise funds for a yeshivah he hoped to establish in Jerusalem—a project he never fulfilled. He returned to the Land of Israel in 1738, settling in Safed. During his travels, he had the opportunity to share his views with the various communities he visited.

His major literary work was entitled *Mishnat Hakhamim* (*The Teachings of Our Sages*). The most extensive section of the book dealt with *emunat hakhamim*, "faith in our Sages." His premise was that Judaism rested on the authority of the rabbinic tradition and that Jews must have faith in the wisdom and truthfulness of the rabbinic Sages. While he recognized that even rabbis can make mistakes in judgment, he argued that the great Sages of the Jewish tradition made very few errors. Although individual rabbis could err, the consensus of rabbinic tradition was true and binding on the faithful. He called on the rabbis of his generation to preach on the basic topic of faith in our Rabbis. All other Jewish teachings were ultimately dependent on this fundamental principle.[6]

While Rabbi Hagiz did not favor teaching Kabbalah to the masses, he nevertheless acknowledged its centrality to Judaism. The elite students who attained a true understanding of Kabbalah could distill its essential ideas to the public in terms the uninitiated could comprehend. He rejected philosophy as a valid source of truth; rather it is the Torah and rabbinic tradition that are the sources of genuine truth.[7]

The midrashic/kabbalistic view, as expressed by Rabbi Hagiz, called on Jews to follow the teachings of the Sages as the best and safest way to remain within the religious fold. To question rabbinic authority would undermine Jewish tradition as a whole.

This strategy essentially called on individuals to surrender their philosophical/rational propensities in favor of an obedient veneration of rabbinic authority. A community based on the midrashic/kabbalistic view tends to conformity of thought and practice; to simple, unquestioning piety; to a sense of satisfaction that it is on the true path in the service of God. Such a single-minded strategy was particularly appealing to those living in confusing times, and the period following the Sabbatai Sevi fiasco was certainly a time of spiritual trauma and confusion. Midrashic/kabbalistic Judaism offered a comprehensive view of life, a virtually infallible rabbinic tradition that answered all questions. It did not demand—or desire—philosophical quests or original theories. Its prized virtue was faithful obedience.

The midrashic/kabbalistic outlook that prevailed by the early eighteenth century continued to hold sway among the masses of Ottoman Jewry for the following generations. Rabbi Eliezer Papo (1785–1828) of Sarajevo, a prolific and highly influential author, reinforced the importance of obedience to rabbinic authority:

> A person should annul his opinion before those greater than him in wisdom and authority, even if it appears to him that they are straying from the path of reason. One should suspect that it is he who is erring.... If one followed their words and this led to something wrong, one will not be punished for [having followed them]; on the contrary, he will receive good reward for his work, since he did what he was supposed to have done.[8]

Rabbi Papo taught that just as there is no change in God and no change in the words of the Torah, so there is no change in the words of our sages. The words of the ancient Rabbis were binding for all times. The holy Rabbis in the earlier generations through the time of the Talmud were imbued with the spirit of God, they were made wise by the hand of God over them; "all of their words were stated with divine inspiration. With their understanding, they foresaw [the needs] of all future generations."[9]

This worldview found a particularly receptive audience among the poorer and less educated group of Jews. Fundamentalism provided a simpler mindset than critical analysis and nuanced readings of sacred texts. But this worldview also prevailed among the more affluent and better educated members of the community as well. They too were spiritually receptive to a worldview that was calming and reassuring, anchored in an authoritative rabbinic tradition.

What were some of the ideas that flowed from the midrashic/ kabbalistic outlook, and how did these ideas manifest themselves in the behavior of the Sephardim in the post–Sabbatai Sevi era?

Otherworldliness

One of the most popular books in the period following Sabbatai Sevi was *Hemdat ha-Yamim*, a work that discussed the laws and customs of the Sabbath and holy days. Published anonymously, this book reflected the midrashic/kabbalistic view of Judaism in an engaging style. It drew on the teachings of the *Zohar*, Lurianic Kabbalah, and the works of kabbalistic ethics written by Rabbi Eliyahu de Vidas and others.

One of its central assumptions was that the spiritual world-to-come was vastly more significant than the material world of human history. Earthly life is short compared to the eternal life of the next world. We are put on earth for a brief time in order to serve God, redeem the sparks of holiness, and gain merit for our souls so that they may be blessed in the world-to-come. In the words of *Hemdat ha-Yamim*:

> This is a warning to Jews to be holy and to be separated from matters of loving this world; and to sanctify themselves and to cling to the love of the Blessed One, to serve Him

and to bless His name, and to keep His commandments
and statutes with desire and love. For what is [the point] of
man's [concern] with this world and its good things?[10]

Indeed, *Hemdat ha-Yamim* teaches that one should not exert
too much time and effort on earning a livelihood. Rather, one
should devote only as much as is needed to make a living—not
to accumulate wealth. Since we need to spend every possible
minute serving God and earning our place in the world-to-come,
each moment given to worldly matters diverts us from our true
goal in life.

It is not fitting for a person to go to his daily labor and work
more than is needed for his sustenance…. It is not fitting
[for one] to work and worry about a world that is not his.
What has he gained from all the work he performed under
the sun? He [truly] has from this world only that which he
sanctifies and separates from this-worldly matters, and
clings to his Master, the Rock who made him.[11]

Hemdat ha-Yamim's disdain for excessive involvement in worldly
business obviously was not conducive to encouraging economic
activity and wealth accumulation among Jews. Whether one was
rich or poor really did not matter in the ultimate scheme of things.
What mattered was whether one was living a righteous, pious life
that would lead to blessing in the eternal spiritual world beyond.

The view of *Hemdat ha-Yamim* was shared by Rabbi Moshe
Hayyim Luzzatto (1707–47), who authored a number of very popular books of Jewish ethics. In the opening chapter of his classic
Mesillat Yesharim, he makes it clear that the duty of human beings
is to serve God so as to earn a worthy place in the world-to-come.

Therefore, man was placed in this world first, so that by
these means [the fulfillment of mitzvot] which were provided for him here, he would be able to reach the place

which had been prepared for him, the world-to-come, there
to be sated with the goodness which he acquired through
them.... A man was created not for his station in this world,
but for his station in the world-to-come. It is only that his
station in this world is a means towards his station in the
world-to-come, which is the ultimate goal.[12]

The midrashic/kabbalistic viewpoint was most successfully
popularized by Rabbi Yaacov Huli and his successors in the classic
biblical/rabbinic folk encyclopedia *Me'am Lo'ez*. Rabbi Huli
(1689–1732), unlike most of his earlier and contemporary rabbinic colleagues, chose to compose his work in the vernacular
Ladino rather than in Hebrew. He was clearly aiming his work for
the Sephardic masses who could not read Hebrew texts with
proper comprehension. The *Me'am Lo'ez* was framed as a biblical
commentary, but included Talmudic and midrashic stories, ethical
teachings, laws, and customs. It was written in a congenial style, so
much so that Rabbi Huli worried that people would read the book
for entertainment rather than for serious Torah study. When the
first volume was published in Istanbul in 1730, it became an immediate success. The *Me'am Lo'ez* went into many editions and was read
enthusiastically by a large audience. It was the single most influential work among the speakers of Judeo-Spanish, certainly through
the latter half of the nineteenth century. More than any other publication of its time, it "canonized" midrashic/kabbalistic Judaism
among the Sephardic masses. Rabbi Huli completed the volume on
B'reishit (Genesis) and much of *Sh'mot* (Exodus). When he died in
1732, other rabbis continued his work and issued volumes completing the Five Books of Moses and other biblical works as well.[13]

On the verse of *B'reishit* 2:7, Rabbi Huli elaborates on thirty
principles relating to the human soul.[14] He begins this section by
stating:

A man must bear in mind that he was created out of nothing and without any merit of his own, only because God

wanted to favor him. The reason why the soul is sent down is to equip man with the necessary knowledge so that he may deserve to return to *Gan Eden* [i.e., the Garden of Eden, heaven] through his own efforts.

A few paragraphs later, he informs readers that God made it possible for us to share God's Holy Law that guides us in the right path "so that we be worthy of learning the happiness promised us in the World-to-Come." Our focus must be on attaining merit for our souls so as to enjoy the blessings of the next world. Mundane concerns are of much less significance. Therefore "you must not be too greedy to save much money, and once you have enough to live in the world with honor and decorum, do not think about getting richer."

The midrashic/kabbalistic approach to Judaism was virtually unopposed among Ottoman Jewry from the latter seventeenth through the mid-nineteenth centuries. It pervaded all strata of Sephardic society and obviously influenced the Jews' patterns of thought and behavior. If Jews declined economically and politically, their religious worldview played a part in this process. Outsiders may have seen the Jews as being apathetic in the face of economic competition and impervious to their lowly political status. But the Jews would have viewed their situation altogether differently. They were not focused on their mundane status: they were concentrating on the world-to-come. Their greatest rabbis and teachers told them not to pay attention to gathering wealth or attaining earthly power; they should devote themselves to fulfilling mitzvot. Poverty and political humiliation did not matter in the final analysis; life on earth was short and transient, while life in the world-to-come was eternal. The Jews were devoted to a transcendent spiritual vision of life; they could actually feel scorn for those who were "successful" in economic and political life, who sought worldly success rather than devoting themselves to earning merit for the world-to-come. In the words of Rabbi Eliezer Papo: "This is a great principle of Judaism, that a person should not seek extraneous things. He should not be fussy about food or clothing or a beautiful home.... His entire aim should be towards the world-to-come, because his [real] home is there."[15] Rabbi Papo tells his readers that it is not proper to worry about any matter of this world, but only about the concerns of heaven.[16]

Passivity

An offshoot of otherworldliness is a spirit of passivity, almost fatalism, in facing the problems of this world. It was considered a great virtue to accept suffering as a sign of God's love, that is, God was punishing us for our sins in this world so we would have greater merit in the world-to-come.

Rabbi Moshe Hagiz taught, for example, that poverty is actually a benefit, since it induces humility and a tendency to turn one's eyes to heaven for assistance.[17] Wealth and poverty are distributed by God, for God's own reasons. Jews were to accept God's decrees and make the best of them. Rabbi Hagiz praised the Jews as the one nation that is able to receive hardships patiently and in a spirit of repentance. Other nations could not survive such sufferings. The Jews were purified by their hardships and will ultimately be well rewarded for their patience and piety.

The extreme level of acceptance and passivity advocated by Rabbi Hagiz is exemplified by the following case. If a non-Jew should come up to a Jew and spit in his face and humiliate him, how should the Jew react? Rabbi Hagiz wrote that the Jew should suffer this humiliation patiently, assuming that it had come to him as a result of his sins. He should therefore confess and repent, recognizing that this terrible incident had occurred as a punishment from God. A pious person should accustom himself not to respond to those who taunt or strike him. Rather, he should accept chastisements and sufferings calmly, with a cheerful countenance.[18] In the eyes of God, it is the oppressed—not the oppressor—who is beloved and cherished. It is the oppressed—not the oppressor—who will be rewarded in the world-to-come.

Rabbi Yaacov Huli reminded his readers that even if a person lost all his capital "he must accept his calamity submissively and bear it with patience, realizing that whatever God decides He does it for the man's own good."[19] Likewise, Jews needed an attitude of quiet resignation in the face of the non-Jewish rulers who had power over them. Being in exile, the Jews were obligated to accept their servile position, humbly recognizing that this was God's will. Jews in exile, like a reed in the wind, needed to bend their heads in order to survive. They should be as quiet and inconspicuous as possible.[20]

This attitude was also advocated by Rabbi Eliezer Papo in his popular ethical tract *Pele Yoetz*. He echoed the belief that whatever happened was for the best, since it was God's will. Suffering and adversity were to be accepted with equanimity, since they provided opportunities to demonstrate true faith in God and to engage in repentance for one's sins.

A striking example of this outlook is found in Rabbi Papo's discussion of marriage.[21] He wrote that if a man had married a woman who turned out to be querulous and unpleasant, he should not therefore separate from her. Rather, he should treat her well and calmly accept any abuse she heaped on him. By suffering from her in this world, the man would thereby earn greater blessings in the world-to-come. Rabbi Papo went so far as to suggest that it was actually preferable to have a miserable wife, if a man felt able to live with this challenge without being led to anger or other sins. Likewise, advised Rabbi Papo, a woman who had married a boorish husband should suffer in silence, without complaint. While she should pray to the Almighty to help her husband change his ways, she should recognize that her unpleasant situation had been destined by heaven.

Similarly, Rabbi Papo thought it wrong to be overly concerned with business matters. Yes, one needed to earn a living to support one's family, but success or failure in business was determined by God. God would provide us with whatever amount God thinks we require—whether much or little. Since we may not rely on miracles, we should engage in some work each day in the hope that the Almighty will bless us with prosperity. But we should devote as much time as possible to more important things, that is, the study of Torah and fulfillment of mitzvot. Spending too much time on attaining income is neither useful nor wise.[22]

Repentance

The prevailing spiritual approach stressed the theme of repentance as a way of purifying one's soul so as to be worthy of blessing in the world-to-come. People were encouraged to undertake rigorous programs of penitence, including inflicting physical pain on themselves. *Hemdat ha-Yamim* recorded the pious deeds of repentance performed by the righteous Jews in the Holy Land, especially during the season before Rosh Hashanah and Yom Kippur. They would remove their usual clothing and wear sackcloth from head to toe. They would take a large stone and pound it against their hearts, then fall to the ground and have others throw small stones at them. This procedure was symbolic of "death by stoning" prescribed by the Torah for heinous sins. Three or four drops of hot wax would then be dripped on them so that they were scalded, symbolic of "death by fire." The penitent would lie on the ground as others pushed and dragged him. The sage conducting this process would say in a mournful voice: "Such should be done to a person who has angered his Creator, such should be done to a person who has provoked his Creator. Woe unto us on the day of judgment, woe unto us on the day of chastisement." Onlookers would then cry, along with the penitent himself. The rabbi would pray that these sufferings be accepted by the Almighty as perfect repentance for any sins that may have been committed by the penitent.[23]

Professor Joseph Dan has indicated that medieval pietists had recommended torture as a means of repentance for those guilty of major sins. The mystics of sixteenth-century Safed, though, expanded this form of repentance for everyone—even the righteous.

The radical new idea that emerged in Safed was that penitence should be a way of life, completely independent of one's sins. Even if an individual had not sinned, somewhere or sometime, someone else certainly had. Jews were collectively responsible for each other, and repentance was a duty that transcended any particular individual. This notion of repentance became an essential feature of the midrashic/kabbalistic worldview.

As mentioned above, Jews were expected to view their misfortunes as punishments from the Almighty for their sins. They were to accept their sufferings with resignation, even cheerfulness. These adversities were to stimulate them to undertake repentance.

A dramatic illustration of this attitude relates to the blood libel of 1840 on the Island of Rhodes. (A blood libel also occurred in Damascus in 1840.) In the spring of that year, some Greek Christians in Rhodes accused a Jew of kidnapping and murdering a Christian child. The police imprisoned the Jew and tried to force him to implicate other Jews as participants in the crime. On Purim eve, the police arrested ten Jewish leaders, including the chief rabbi, Michael Yaacov Israel. The victims were tortured, and draconian measures were ordered against the entire Jewish community. The Jewish quarter was blockaded, and no food was allowed into the area for three days.

In Europe, leaders attempted to save the Jews of Rhodes and Damascus. Moses Montefiore and Adolphe Cremieux were at the head of these efforts. Montefiore was received by Sultan Abdul Medjid in Istanbul on October 28, 1840 (after the Jews in Rhodes had already been released from prison and absolved of the charges against them). The sultan issued a decree declaring the innocence of the Jews of Damascus and Rhodes and stated that the Turkish government would not allow its Jewish subjects to be tormented by such accusations.

Rabbi Michael Yaacov Israel, who was among those imprisoned and tortured in Rhodes, preached a sermon on the Sabbath before Passover in 1840, shortly after he and the other Jewish leaders had been freed from prison. In his sermon, he referred to the horrifying events just experienced by him and his community. Expressing bitterness that the Rhodian officials had given credence to the blood libel, he then proceeded to give his congregation words of religious chastisement:

> You know about all the suffering which we underwent due to this blood libel, instigated by wicked non-Jews. We are brought low as dust. We are struck and oppressed.... Woe unto us for what has happened. Our sins brought this on, for everything is from God, may His name be blessed. This evil befell us because of our many sins.... Our sages have truly taught that no evil descends from Heaven. All God's actions are for the good. Even though a person may see something which appears to be bad, when he thinks about it he will realize that it is good. For the moment it may appear that something is bad and that all the sufferings that befall the Jews are bad, but in the end everything is for our own good, in order to have us turn in repentance.[24]

Exterior World, Interior World

We began this chapter with comments by outside observers concerning Jewish life in the Ottoman Empire during the eighteenth and early nineteenth centuries. They described the Jews as apathetic, uncompetitive, and passive in the face of insult and abuse. Indeed, any objective study of the Jews of the period will verify that there was a pronounced economic, political, and cultural decline and that many Jews did appear apathetic in the face of their troubles.

But we have also seen that the spiritual worldview promoted by the rabbinic leadership fostered otherworldliness, passivity, piety, repentance, and disdain for too much involvement in business. Jews who heeded the advice of their rabbis—and we may assume that many did during the period under discussion—would have described their conditions in more favorable terms. Yes, they suffered poverty and humiliation, but these were unimportant in the overall scheme of things. Earthly life was insignificant compared to the eternal life of the next world. Their sufferings on earth were a means of purifying their souls so that they would be worthy of great reward in the world-to-come. If their economic and political situation deteriorated, this was the will of God. They accepted God's chastisements with equanimity—even joy— as a sign of their true faith. Economic development was not a priority for them; rather, they were taught to be far more concerned with their spiritual treasures than their ephemeral worldly assets. If non-Jews taunted them, Jews did not lower themselves to respond, any more than they would respond to a barking dog. It was the oppressor—not the oppressed—who was guilty in the eyes of God. The oppressor was to be ignored and despised, while the oppressed kept their pure faith in God and God's ultimate justice. Whatever evil befell the Jews, they could be sure it was due to their own sins, as a means of prodding them to repentance.

Thus, the masses of Jews could make peace with their sufferings. Their rabbis and teachers offered them an authoritative midrashic/kabbalistic view of Judaism that addressed their needs. If their exterior conditions appeared lowly and degraded, their inner life was rich and resplendent.

The deterioration of the Jewish position was the result of many factors: despondency after Sabbatai Sevi's failure, the general decline of the Ottoman Empire, increased competition from Greeks and Armenians, wars and rebellions, and so on. But surely the Jews' own attitudes contributed to the worsening of their economic and political status. It is impossible to know exactly to what extent external conditions influenced rabbinic leaders to espouse an otherworldly philosophy. Likewise, it is impossible to determine to what extent that philosophy contributed to the deterioration in the conditions of the Jews. It is fair to say, though, that both external and internal factors were at work.

Negative Consequences of Jewish Otherworldliness

We have pointed out the positive features of Jewish otherworldliness. The Jews had a cohesive and meaningful structure for understanding their lives, for coping with their miseries, and for maintaining inner strength and dignity in the face of so many difficulties.

Yet the midrashic/kabbalistic worldview, while focusing on the blessings of the next world, engendered negative consequences for Jews in this world. Jews were asked to suspend their own power of reason, to accept the tales and miracles of rabbinic and kabbalistic literature as being literally true, to rely on rabbinic authority with total faith. This approach fostered a narrowing of the boundaries of intellectual discussion. It tended to conformity of thought and action, to disdain for alternate views and opinions. It did not foster creativity and original thinking.

This attitude relegated power and prestige to rabbis and teachers, in their roles as the authoritative interpreters of traditional religious wisdom. While individuals of great intellect and high idealism were attracted to the rabbinate, less talented men were also drawn to this field. A man of mediocre abilities might choose to be a rabbi or teacher as a means of gaining status or because other economic options were limited and unattractive. Thus, authority sometimes fell into the hands of those who were not capable of handling it. The lamentable state of education among the Jews of Turkey through the latter nineteenth century was in part due to the unsatisfactory quality of teachers and rabbinic leaders.

A fundamentalist viewpoint, steeped in midrashic/kabbalistic lore, can easily slip into the realm of superstition. Maimonides—the champion of the philosophical/rational Jewish tradition—was, of course, vehemently opposed to anything that smacked of superstition. The midrashic/kabbalistic approach, though, invited the growth of superstition. After all, the Midrash and Kabbalah were full of information about spirits and demons, angels and souls. The boundary between earthly life and the world of spirits was porous. To accept these texts as literally true was to be receptive to the belief in the evil eye, demons, and other supernatural forces. Since these metaphysical powers were ubiquitous, people needed to protect themselves by means of magical incantations, blue beads, potions, etc. A host of superstitious beliefs and practices became rooted within Jewish life, some borrowed from the Muslims and Christians of the empire. When it came to warding off evil spirits, adherents of all three religions engaged in superstitious practices—and no doubt learned techniques from one another.

The midrashic/kabbalistic approach fostered negative attitudes toward business. The rabbis assured their followers that economic success in this world was not nearly as important as leading a pious life that would be rewarded in the world-to-come. They encouraged people to work as few hours as possible, so as to be able to devote more time to the study of Torah and the performance of mitzvot. This advice had serious negative consequences not just for Jewish involvement in business, but for their spiritual condition as well.

In the problematic economic climate of the Ottoman Empire, workers seldom had the luxury of having employment that would allow them to work for a few hours and then free them for Torah study and mitzvot for the rest of the day. To run a successful business or to hold a lucrative job, one had to devote oneself to one's work. Those not ready or able to engage seriously in business slipped to the lower rungs of the economic ladder. Large numbers of Jews indeed found themselves working at menial jobs. Since these jobs paid so little, Jewish laborers actually had to spend more time at their work just to eke out a meager living. A result of the general process of economic erosion among Jews was a concomitant erosion in the level of education attained by their children. Since the fathers earned so little, children had to find work to bolster the families' income. By age thirteen or fourteen, many boys had to drop out of school in order to work. Since they were so young and had so little education, they ended up working in petty jobs that offered little hope for advancement. A vicious cycle of poverty and ignorance had taken hold—much to the detriment of the physical and spiritual conditions of the Jews.

As already noted, passivity in the face of abuse was another virtue encouraged by the midrashic/kabbalistic approach. Although turning the other cheek may indeed be a great moral virtue, negative consequences result from it. A victim who does not defend him or herself is more likely to be victimized again. By accepting abuse passively, Jews were actually encouraging further attacks on themselves. Non-Jews quickly realized that they could commit indignities against Jews without fear of reprisal. Even children could attack Jews with disdain. To be sure, it is morally superior to be oppressed rather than to be the oppressor; yet, these are not the only alternatives. If Jews had been encouraged to fight back and to defend their honor, they may have prevented future attacks against themselves. The antagonists would know that they could not abuse Jews without paying a heavy price in return.

The deeply held assumptions of the midrashic/kabbalistic Judaism of Ottoman Jewry were to prevail through the latter nineteenth century and even into the early twentieth century. Before considering how the Sephardim handled their confrontation with the tide of modernity, let us look more deeply into their inner lives, as reflected in their rabbinic works in Ladino, their family and communal patterns, their customs and folkways.

7

The Religious/Social
Structure of Life

By the early eighteenth century, the masses of Sephardim could not read Hebrew works with much comprehension. The Hebrew skills of the men were adequate for the recitation of their prayers and for following the Torah readings in the synagogue. The Hebrew skills of the women were significantly less. Thus, the masses were largely cut off from access to the vast rabbinic and general literature composed in the Hebrew language over the ages. Even the Hebrew works authored by Sephardic sages of the Ottoman Empire did not reach most Sephardim directly, but through the translations and interpretations of their rabbis and teachers.

Some works in Ladino, printed in Rashi script, had been published during the sixteenth and seventeenth centuries. In 1550, *Hovot ha-Levavot*, the classic ethical work by the medieval Sephardic rabbi Bahya ibn Pakuda, was published in Istanbul in a translation by Zadik ben Yosef Formon. It was reprinted in 1569. In 1568, a Ladino translation of extracts of the *Shulhan Arukh* was published in Salonika. During the sixteenth century, the Jewish presses in Istanbul and Salonika issued several other publications in Ladino: laws of ritual slaughter of animals (1510), Psalms with Ladino translation (1540), Torah with Ladino translation (1547), the Later Prophets with Ladino translation (1568), and *Livro Yihus haTsadikim* (c. 1593), a book celebrating the righteousness of various rabbinic sages. There were also a number of Spanish language works in Latin letters issued by the Jewish presses in Amsterdam, Venice, and Ferrara, although these had limited impact on the communities in the Ottoman Empire.

Rabbi Yaacov Huli gave a tremendous impetus to publications in Ladino when he issued the first volume of *Me'am Lo'ez* in 1730. He sensed that the Judeo-Spanish-speaking Jews needed religious texts in the language they understood. The popularity of this work proved that Rabbi Huli's intuition had been correct: the public longed for religious instruction in their own vernacular language.

A twentieth-century Salonika-born scholar, Rabbi Michael Molho, wrote an appreciation of the *Me'am Lo'ez*:

> The *Me'am Lo'ez* is varied, rich, profound in its contents. It deals with the institutions of Judaism, its ceremonies, its rites, its ethics, its philosophy, its rules, its history.... This heap of notions is strung together with the golden thread of anecdotes, legends, and historical accounts and folklore. Nothing of affectation, gravity, pretentiousness. A stream of naturalness crosses its pages which have throughout the tone of a familiar chat, of an amusing story. No apparent didacticism or erudite mannerisms. It is a friend that leads by the hand, teaches you, amuses you, invites you to laugh and at times excites you emotionally and makes you cry. It enthralls and holds the attention of the least curious among its readers or listeners.[1]

Upon Huli's death in 1732, other authors continued the project through the eighteenth and nineteenth centuries in his style, so as to produce volumes on all five books of the Torah, Joshua, Isaiah, Song of Songs, Ruth, Ecclesiastes, Esther, Job, and Daniel. Huli's successors were Rabbis Yitzhak Magriso, Yitzhak Argueti, Menahem Mitrani, Yitzhak Yehudah Aba, Nessim Moshe Abad, and Hayyim Yitzhak Sciaky.

In the introduction to the *Me'am Lo'ez*, Rabbi Huli presented four fundamental principles of Judaism: (1) that God created the world, guides it, rewards the righteous and punishes the wicked; (2) that God gave the people of Israel the Written Torah and the Oral Torah, which together teach Jews their obligations; (3) that God commanded us to love our neighbors as ourselves; (4) that each person must contemplate his mortality, thereby recognizing the foolishness of following the ways of sinfulness. Thus, Jews must observe the religious precepts carefully, so as to be worthy of God's blessings. Rabbi Huli wanted his readers to know that they could improve themselves by devotion to their religious traditions.

He knew that many of his readers were poor and intellectually unsophisticated. He wanted to instill within them feelings of self-worth, a belief that they could serve God admirably in spite of their particular shortcomings. The virtues of sincerity and righteousness could be attained even by simple people. Piety was more important than intellectual achievements. The Bible did not praise the prophets for their wisdom or scholarship but for their moral qualities. Noah was not saved because of his learning, but because he was righteous. God praised Moses for his humility. God commanded us to be upright (*Sh'mot* 18:24–25).[2]

God wants us to serve God with a pure, honest heart. A good-hearted person will be forgiven for occasional sins. However, a mean-spirited person is morally blemished, so that even his or her good deeds are flawed (*B'reishit* 14:13).

The *Me'am Lo'ez* reflected sympathy toward the poor and downtrodden. Rabbi Huli cited religious texts that extolled humility and honest labor. Our level of material prosperity is dependent on God's will, and we must accept our economic condition as God-given. We can devote ourselves to righteousness, regardless of our economic status. We should work to earn an honest living and not look down on any honest occupation. Nor should we attempt to live in a style beyond what we can afford (*B'reishit* 28:22).

In God's eyes, the wealthy are not more important than the poor. In many cases, God is even more responsive to the prayers of the poor, since they pray with tears and sincere emotion (*B'reishit* 19:27). The wealthy are obligated to share their material blessings with the poor (*B'reishit* 14:20 and 14:22). Moral virtue is far more significant than material wealth. To be compassionate, humble, upright, and merciful are the true goals of a good human being (*B'reishit* 18:1).

God created Adam from dust, not from gold (*B'reishit* 2:7). People should learn humility from this. Humility is the foundation for every other proper moral quality. Even when a person has great material status and feels like the "stars of the sky," he or she must stay humble as the "sand on the seashore" (*B'reishit* 22:18). One who is small in this world will be great in the world-to-come, and one who considers oneself great in this world will be small in the world-to-come (*B'reishit* 23:1).

One must be humble, even in his or her religious observances. One should not flaunt his or her piety, but rather should attempt to conceal it (*B'reishit* 21:33).

Rabbi Huli and his successors were deeply steeped in the midrashic/kabbalistic view of Judaism.[3] Their thousands of readers were guided in this worldview that stressed rabbinic authority, observance of Halakhah, devotion to Kabbalah, and focus on the blessings of the world-to-come. The *Me'am Lo'ez* valued obedient faith rather than rational philosophical inquiry; passive acceptance of God's decrees rather than active involvement to change the status quo; traditionalism rather than innovation.

By writing in the vernacular Ladino, Rabbi Huli demonstrated his commitment to provide religious guidance for the masses of Sephardim of Judeo-Spanish background. Other authors followed his example by publishing works in Ladino. Between 1731 and 1807, the Jewish press in Istanbul issued seventy-eight books in Hebrew and thirty in Ladino.[4] Rabbi Abraham Asa issued a Ladino translation of the Bible, published between 1739 and 1744, that used contemporary Ladino rather than the archaic form of the language utilized in earlier translations. Rabbi Asa also translated other Hebrew works into Ladino: selections of the *Shulhan Arukh* (1749), the ethical work *Menorat ha-Maor* by Rabbi Yitzhak Aboab (1762); and a compilation of Jewish laws (1733).[5] Other Ladino works included tracts of Jewish ethics, prayer books with Ladino translations, and religious poetry. (By the mid-nineteenth century, a secular Ladino literature was also emerging: newspapers, novels, short stories, poetry. This phenomenon will be discussed in a later chapter.)

We see, then, that a religious Ladino literature was widely available within the Judeo-Spanish communities. Through the mid-nineteenth century, this literature was essentially rooted in the midrashic/kabbalistic worldview, with little available dealing with philosophy or general topics unrelated to religion.

Rabbinic Leadership

Since the Judeo-Spanish Sephardim constituted a traditional religious community, they naturally turned to their rabbis as their religious authorities. Sephardic Jewry produced learned rabbinic leaders who studied in the yeshivot in Istanbul, Salonika, Izmir, Rhodes, Jerusalem, and other cities. Through the modern period, Sephardic rabbis of the Ottoman Empire published a significant literature—responsa, rabbinic commentaries, sermons, ethical tracts, and kabbalistic works. A perusal of their publications reveals their extensive knowledge of the classic sources of biblical and rabbinic literature.

It must be remembered that Judeo-Spanish civilization produced rabbinic luminaries whose works have had a lasting and continuing impact on Jewish life. Among the mainstays of halakhic literature are such Sephardic sages as rabbis Yosef Karo (*Beit Yosef, Shulhan Arukh,* responsa); David ibn Abi Zimra, Shemuel de Medina, Barukh Angel (responsa); Hayyim Benveniste (*Kenesset ha-Gedolah*); Hayyim Yosef David Azulai, Israel Moshe Hazan, Hayyim Palache, Eliyahu Hazan, Benzion Uziel, Hayyim David Halevy (responsa and other halakhic works); Hayyim Hizkiya Medini (*Sedei Hemed*). The Israel family of the Island of Rhodes produced learned rabbis and authors from the early eighteenth through the mid-twentieth centuries. The chief rabbi of the Land of Israel under Ottoman rule (known by the title of *Rishon le-Zion*), beginning with Rabbi Moshe Angel Galante (1620–89) and going through Rabbi Benzion Uziel (1880–1953), was invariably a Sephardic rabbi of the Judeo-Spanish tradition.[6]

The Judeo-Spanish communities also produced authors of classic works in Kabbalah and ethics. Among them were the outstanding sages of sixteenth-century Safed, including rabbis Moshe Cordovero, Hayyim Vital, Eliyahu de Vidas, Moshe Alsheikh, Eliezer Azikri, Shelomo Alkabets—indeed the entire circle surrounding Rabbi Yitzhak Luria. Subsequent generations of Sephardic authors of classic works of Jewish ethics included rabbis Hayyim David Azulai (*Lev David*), Eliyahu ha-Cohen (*Shevet Musar*), Hayyim Palache (*Kaf ha-Hayyim*), and Eliezer Papo (*Pele Yoetz*). Judeo-Spanish-speaking scholars filled the numerous academies scattered throughout the Ottoman Empire, teaching Torah to many thousands of students during the course of well over four centuries. Hundreds of books of Jewish learning were authored by these sages on the broad range of Torah scholarship.

Sephardic rabbis were known by various titles, each of which sheds light on the rabbinic role. A popular title was *marbits Torah*, one who disseminated the teachings of the Torah to his community.[7] The rabbi was expected to be learned, well-versed in everything related to religious life. He often headed or served on the community's rabbinic court. He taught Jewish law and tradition to his community through his public lectures, classes, and periodic sermons (usually delivered on the Shabbat before Passover, the Shabbat before Yom Kippur, and on other special occasions) and might also teach in the city's yeshivot. Rabbis supervised activities relating to kosher food, schools, the building and maintaining of ritual baths, and other assorted responsibilities.

Sephardic rabbis were also known by the title *haham*, wise man. Aside from knowledge of the whole range of Torah studies, the rabbi was expected to be "wise," to understand the needs of his community, to offer personal guidance to those in need of his wisdom. The *haham* provided moral instruction, advice on methods of repentance, and guidance on how to cope with life's problems and challenges.

The close involvement of the rabbis in the daily lives of their communities may have generated an increased understanding of their needs and sympathy for their struggles. This heightened rabbinic sensitivity may have influenced the Sephardic approach to Halakhah. Rabbi Hayyim Yosef David Azulai (1724–1806) cited the opinion of Rabbi Yosef Shemuel Cazes of Mantua, who believed that Sephardic sages tended to the quality of *hesed*, compassion, and therefore were lenient in Halakhah.[8]

Another title by which rabbis were known was *haver ha'ir*, "friend" of the city. The word *haver* has the connotation of a distinguished or exceptionally pious person, as well as implying friendship. The rabbi was expected to be saintly and righteous. He was also expected to be a "friend," that is, someone genuinely concerned with the well-being of the people, not aloof or self-righteous. Rabbi Hayyim Palache of nineteenth-century Izmir used to bless the members of his community at the conclusion of prayer services, to indicate his respect for them and his hope that the Almighty would bless them with all good things. Rabbis presided over the religious ceremonies of the life cycle, celebrating with the people in times of joy and mourning with them in times of grief. It was not uncommon for rabbis to participate in reading the synagogue prayer services, including reading the Torah portion. Rabbis recognized their responsibility for the total religious and spiritual welfare of their community. They did not live a life removed from the everyday needs of their people.

The rabbi was, in many cases, the official representative of the Jewish community to the government officials and to other non-Jewish leaders. The rabbi was the symbol of the Jewish community to the outside world.

Various customs arose concerning the community's relationship with its rabbi. When a rabbi was called for an *aliyah* to the Torah, the entire congregation stood up as a sign of respect. They remained standing until the rabbi recited the blessing at the conclusion of the reading of his Torah portion. In some communities, it was customary for people to kiss the rabbi's hand or the sleeve of his robe, after which the rabbi would utter a blessing. Some had the custom of visiting the graves of deceased rabbis as a sign of ongoing respect. They prayed that the Almighty would have mercy on them, based on the merit of the holy rabbis who had passed on to the next world.

The Family

The traditional family life was patriarchal. The husband/father was head of the household and was honored accordingly. Nonetheless, the wife/mother—although formally subservient in status to her husband—was often the guiding spirit of family life and either made or participated in the important decisions. A husband usually addressed his wife in the formal second person plural form of Judeo-Spanish. In turn, the wife addressed her husband in the respectful third person singular.

It was customary for children to kiss the hands of both father and mother, especially on the eves of the Sabbath and festivals, and to receive a blessing from them. Likewise, they kissed the hands of grandparents and were blessed by them.

Children were generally named after their grandparents or other relatives, even when these namesakes were alive. Traditionally, the first-born son and daughter were named after the father's parents; the second-born son and daughter were named after the mother's parents. Subsequent children were named after other relatives, alternating between the father's and mother's side of the family. This custom was a means for children to honor their parents by naming their own children after them. A sense of family solidarity and continuity was reinforced. It was common for grandparents to have a number of grandchildren bearing their names. By having members of the new generation bear the names of their elders, the generations of the family felt a deep bond.

When a man was called for an *aliyah* to the Torah in the synagogue, his younger relatives would rise in respect and remain standing for the reading of his Torah portion. Aside from being a sign of honor for the person called to the Torah, this custom also tended to tie family members together. The standing relatives felt a special connection between them. Their family had been honored; they were proud to be part of the family.

The first-born child of a family was called by the honorific title *bohor* (first-born male) or *bohora* (first-born female). This title sometimes was used with the given name and sometimes in place of the given name. Thus, my grandfather was known as Bohor Yehuda Angel and also as Bohor Angel. First-born children were also respectfully referred to as *hermano* (brother) or *hermana* (sister) by their younger siblings.

In keeping with the Jewish tradition of respecting elders, younger people would direct their eyes downward when speaking to elders. It was considered disrespectful to look an elder in the eye, since this implied an equal relationship. By looking down, the younger person thereby showed proper deference.[9] Younger people did not address elders by their first names, but rather with honorific titles: *senyor* (mister), *senyora* (madam), *tio* (uncle), *tia* (aunt).

Education

Until the mid-nineteenth century, few girls received formal education in schools. Most girls learned what they needed to know from their mothers and other female relatives—grandmothers, aunts, older sisters—and sometimes also from tutors. They were instructed in domestic skills such as cooking and sewing. Some learned to read and write in Ladino, with a few also learning rudimentary Hebrew. They learned some Hebrew prayers and blessings by heart, as well as a repertoire of Ladino prayers and blessings.

Boys attended schools, where they were taught to read and write in Ladino. They studied Hebrew and learned the Torah with its traditional Ladino translation. They also learned rudimentary

skills in mathematics and other subjects that were deemed necessary for the boys' progress in life. When a boy was brought to
school for the first time, his parents and friends would accompany
him. As they left home for school, they would sing a Ladino song:

La Torah, la Torah	The Torah, the Torah
El hijico la dira	The little child will recite it.
Con el pan y el queso	With bread and cheese
Indose para el meldar	He goes to the school,
Encontrose con un malah.	He encounters an angel [or, accompanied by an angel].
Ande vas hijo del Dio?	Where are you going, child of God?
A meldar la ley del Dio.	To study the Torah of God.
Vidas que te de el Dio	May God give you life
A ti y a tu padre	You and your father
Y a todos los gidios.[10]	And all the Jews.

The traditional school, known as the *meldar* (i.e., place to
read, to study), emphasized rote study. Boys learned the prayers
and passages from the Bible in the traditional melodies, chanting
them repeatedly until they knew them by heart. Modernizing educators in the latter nineteenth and early twentieth centuries found
fault with this system. M. Fresco, describing a traditional school in
Istanbul in 1906, lambasted the old-fashioned methodology:

The text and its translation are there to be chanted in
singsong, to be whined, not to be understood. There is
nothing more strange and more ridiculous than to hear
recited in this manner the most vehement prophecies of
Isaiah or Ezekiel, the delicious idyll of Ruth, or the fiery
pages from the Song of Songs.... The children cry out the
verses in high, shrill tones, each trying to outdo the other.
They are accompanied at intervals by the loud, whining
voice of their teacher.[11]

To be sure, the traditional educational system had its faults and could have benefited from a serious overhaul in its curriculum and pedagogical methods. Yet, modern readers need to try to understand these schools on their own terms.

The *meldar* existed for one primary purpose: to train boys in the patterns of traditional Jewish religion. Teachers knew that many of the boys were poor and would not remain in school much past the age of twelve or thirteen. Given its limited time and resources, the *meldar* had to be sure that the boys would "graduate" as literate Jews, that is, with basic knowledge of Jewish religious observances, with fluency in prayers, and with close familiarity with the Bible. Learning by rote—certainly not fashionable in modern educational circles—had its genuine value. The end result of rote study was that almost all Sephardic boys knew their prayers, could function comfortably and happily in their synagogues, and could recite large sections of the Torah and Prophets by heart. Even if many (or even most) could not fully understand the meaning of their recitations, these traditional texts became part and parcel of their personalities and inner lives. In later generations, students who attended modernized schools may have studied the texts with more comprehension and analysis, but they were not necessarily as emotionally attached to the texts as those who studied in the old-fashioned schools.

A relatively small number of boys had the opportunity to continue their studies after they finished with the *meldar*. Wealthier parents could afford to have their sons attend higher-level schools. Sons of rabbis and learned laymen also were encouraged to continue their studies in advanced yeshivot. Yet, until the latter part of the nineteenth century, boys had little opportunity to study subjects outside the realm of traditional religion. Jewish schools functioned in Judeo-Spanish, so that students did not even learn to speak the language of the land—Turkish. It was not until the 1890s that the Jewish community seriously engaged in discussions about adopting Turkish as their mother tongue. The first Jewish association for the propagation of Turkish language was founded in

1890.[12] It was not very successful in gaining widespread support in the Jewish community.

Jewish Neighborhoods

While Jews were not restricted to ghettos in the Ottoman Empire, they had a natural tendency to form Jewish neighborhoods. Religious law necessitated that they live within walking distance of their synagogues. Moreover, religious life was enhanced by densely populated Jewish neighborhoods that could more easily support a network of vital services, such as synagogues, schools, ritual baths, and kosher food establishments. Living in a Jewish neighborhood among relatives and friends provided a warm, friendly environment for life. Sabbaths and festivals were made more joyous by the fact that one's neighbors were also observing these holy days; the neighborhood reinforced Jewish observances and customs. Jewish neighborhoods—where Judeo-Spanish was the dominant language—provided Jews with a feeling of communal belonging.

Jews in the Ottoman Empire generally lived in houses built around a courtyard. In some towns, Jews lived in sections adjacent to Muslim neighborhoods. It became increasingly common in the nineteenth and twentieth centuries for Jewish neighborhoods also to have non-Jewish residents, so that there was some interaction among the groups.[13]

The Synagogue

The synagogue was at the center of religious life. Prayer services were held every day for the morning, afternoon, and evening prayers. Some synagogues were grand buildings, while others were small and quite simple. Synagogues were generally maintained by the community, through a system of internal Jewish taxation. The wealthy paid more, and the poor paid whatever they could afford—if anything. The synagogues also collected contributions from worshipers who received honors, for example, being called to the

Torah, or performing one of the mitzvot relating to removing or returning the Torah scroll to or from the ark. Other contributions were given as memorial offerings or in honor of special occasions.

Women seldom attended synagogue services. When they did, they sat in a section separated from the men.

The synagogue was popularly called *kal* or *kehillah*, meaning "community." It was not seen merely as a house of worship, but as the center of the communal structure. The members of a synagogue were known as *yehidim*, "individuals." This term emphasized the uniqueness of each member and underscored his right to be honored and respected.

While the synagogue was created for the honor of God, it was also the place where individual Jews received honors. Although the wealthier members could expect to have many of these honors, poorer members also could expect to receive them.

Men would be called to the Torah especially when they were observing the anniversary of the death of a parent or other family member. The Torah reader would announce: *Ya'amod hashem hatov ... likro ba-Torah yishmereihu Tsuro* (Let the man of good name, so-and-so, arise to read from the Torah, may the Almighty watch over him). The man singled out for the *aliyah* was referred to as a person of a "good name," that is, a man of stature, worthy of respect. In announcing the name, the Torah reader preceded the name with a title based on the particular person being called. When calling a married man, the title *hagevir* or *ha'adon* would be used; when calling an unmarried man, *habahur* was the usual title. A rabbi would be called with his title: *moreinu harav*, or *he-hakham hashalem*. Honorific titles might also be used when referring to the lay leader of the community or to other distinguished personalities.

When a man's name was announced to be called to the Torah, he was called by his Hebrew name as well as by his family name. In some communities a man was called by his first and last names, and in other communities it was customary to add the name of the person's father as well. It was a point of honor with Sephardim to have their family name used when being called to the Torah. (This differs from the widespread custom among Ashkenazic Jews to be called "so-and-so son of so-and-so," without mentioning the family name.)

When a person called to the Torah proceeded to the reader's desk, congregants would greet him with the word *bekhavod*, "with honor." As he walked through the synagogue hearing this word of recognition, and as he knew that his younger relatives had stood up in his honor, the man certainly felt proud and happy. His sense of dignity was reinforced. At the conclusion of his portion of the Torah reading, he would return to his seat as congregants called out to him: *Hazak uvarukh*, "Be strong and be blessed." He would reply: *Barukh tihyeh*, "May you be blessed," or *Hazak ve'ematz*, "Be strong and of good courage." These salutations were generally accompanied by a Turkish hand gesture known as *temena*, where the person raised his right hand toward his forehead as a sort of salute.

These synagogue customs were reflections of the inner world of the Sephardim, a world where they and their names were valued and honored. It was their own pleasant world, separated from the outside society, which could be harsh and cruel.

Synagogue Music

The *hazzan*, or reader, led the services and was expected to have a pleasant voice. He sang the prayers to their traditional melodies and also introduced new melodies from time to time. Much of the service was sung with the active and enthusiastic participation of the congregation. The distinctive melodies for Shabbat and the various holidays were uplifting and enjoyable.

Rabbi Israel Moshe Hazan (1808–63), born in Izmir, commented on the practice of *hazzanim* to set Jewish prayers to non-Jewish tunes. Some rabbis opposed this practice. Rabbi Hazan, though, had no objection as long as the music added to the beauty and devotion of the synagogue services. He wrote:

> And I call to witness heaven and earth that when I was in
> the great city of sages and scholars, Izmir, I saw among the

illustrious sages those who were great singers according to the art of music. At their head was the illustrious Rabbi Abraham ha-Cohen Arias. For the musical form for the High Holy Days, which requires great submissiveness which is called among them *hizun*, they used to go to the Christian churches on their holy days, [and would stand] behind the wall [so they could hear the church music] in order to learn from [the Christians] the submissive tone which deeply moves the heart. From those melodies, they arranged wondrous *kadishim* and *kedushot* [melodies for the *Kaddish* and the *K'dushah* prayers].[14]

Sephardic *hazzanim* became well versed in the forms of Turkish music and introduced Turkish musical style into the synagogue services. This was also true in the area of *piyyutim*, religious poetry set to music, sung on various occasions in the synagogue and at home. Many of these songs were strongly influenced by Turkish music.[15] This practice seems to have begun very early in the Sephardic experience in the Ottoman Empire. In 1545 (5305), a book was published in Istanbul, entitled *Shirim u-Zemirot ve-Tishbahot*, that included religious poetry by the great Sephardic poets Shelomo ibn Gabirol, Abraham ibn Ezra, and Yehudah Halevy as well as by Rabbi Shelomo ben Mazal Tov, "according to the melody of the Sephardim and the *Yishmaelim* [Muslims]."

Competent laymen with pleasant voices were given the honor of leading prayer services and participating in the singing of the *piyyutim*. They were invited with the word *bekhavod*, "with honor." Thus, the synagogue was a bastion of religious faith and tradition, while at the same time bolstering the sense of honor among its members.

Life Cycle Observances

Lionel Trilling referred to the "half-uttered or unuttered or unutterable expressions of value" that characterize a group's mannerisms, behavior patterns, and outlook on life.[16] Important elements of a group's culture are reflected in their customs and attitudes. Insights into Judeo-Spanish civilization may be gained through a study of its religious and folk traditions.

According to Jewish law, a healthy male child is to be circumcised on the eighth day of life. Among Sephardim, it was customary to have a vigil—known as *shemirah* (watching)—on the night preceding the circumcision.[17] Those who spent the night in the baby's home read a service that included selections from the Bible, Mishnah, Midrash, and *Zohar*. This ceremony was designed to protect the baby from evil spirits that might attempt to harm him. In some communities, a sword was hung in the child's room in order to ward off these spirits. Other items that were deemed effective in averting evil spirits were blue beads and sprigs of rue.

The belief in evil spirits was common among non-Jews of the Ottoman Empire, whether Muslim or Christian; Jews shared this widespread belief in malevolent supernatural spirits. In the case of the *shemirah*, we see an example of the blend of religion and superstition that came to prevail within the Sephardic communities. While the ceremony was meant to fend off evil spirits, the core observance was the reading of sacred religious texts.[18]

Circumcisions generally took place on the morning of the eighth day and were commonly held at the synagogue. In Rhodes and other communities, it was customary for the *kitatha* (godmother) to carry the infant to the synagogue, holding him on a cushion. A joyous retinue of relatives and friends would accompany her, singing and dancing along the way. As the group wended its way to the synagogue, friends and neighbors would call out their words of congratulations and good wishes.

In the synagogue, an ornamental chair—known as the chair of Eliyahu the prophet—was placed on an elevated platform. The *sandak* (godfather) would hold the child on a cushion on his lap during the circumcision. The congregation sang traditional hymns that had been composed especially for the celebration of circumcisions. After the appropriate blessings were recited, the child's name was announced. The assembled group would then enjoy a festive repast.

If the family's house was large enough, the circumcision ceremony would be held at home. Colonel Bernard Rottiers visited the Island of Rhodes in 1828 and described a circumcision party he attended at the home of his Jewish employee. Rottiers wrote that the house was crowded with many relatives and friends. People sat on Turkish-style sofas, ate sweets, and drank excellent wine. The rabbi gave an erudite discourse in honor of the occasion.[19]

On the birth of a daughter, parents invited family and friends to a special banquet, at which the rabbi held the baby and recited a blessing for her good health and happiness. He then announced the girl's name as chosen by her parents. The baby was passed from guest to guest, each of whom wished her and her parents long life and happiness. This ceremony, dating back to Jewish practice in medieval Spain, was known as *las fadas* (the fairies). It grew from the popular belief among Spanish Christians that good fairies attended celebrations of the birth of babies and were expected to give their blessings. The Jews, while substituting people for fairies as the ones to offer blessings, still maintained reference to the fairies in the name of the ceremony.

When a boy reached the age of thirteen, he was deemed to be a bar mitzvah—a man subject to the responsibilities and privileges of observing the commandments of Judaism. The bar mitzvah boy would attend synagogue services on a weekday morning and don tefillin as a sign of his new adulthood. (It was not unusual for boys to start wearing tefillin a month or two before their bar mitzvah, but without reciting the blessing, as a way of accustoming themselves to wrapping the tefillin properly. The blessing was recited for the first time when the boy was thirteen years and one day old, or the next day if the bar mitzvah date fell on Saturday.) The bar mitzvah boy would be congratulated and was treated to a special breakfast at home with family and friends. All in all, the bar mitzvah commemoration was fairly simple. There was no ceremony to commemorate a bat mitzvah, since the bat mitzvah ceremony is essentially a twentieth-century creation.

Early marriages were common among Sephardim until the beginning of the twentieth century. The bride's family was expected to provide a dowry as part of the marriage arrangements. The groom, by means of the Jewish marriage contract (*ketubah*), guaranteed financial security to the bride. Where bride and groom were both from poor families, these financial arrangements were often more symbolic than actual. It was not uncommon for the young couple to begin their married life living in the same home as the groom's parents. They would eventually move into their own home once they started to have children.

On the night before the wedding, the bride would go to the ritual bath accompanied by her mother and other female relatives and friends. The women sang songs and enjoyed sweet pastries. Afterward, they returned to the home of the bride's family, where the celebrations continued.

The groom sent the bride a plate of henna surrounded by lit candles. His parents and friends delivered this gift (and other gifts as well) while singing traditional Ladino wedding songs. The bride, her family, and friends received the gifts and offered sweets to the groom's family and friends.

The wedding ceremony was conducted according to the Sephardic custom and sung in the traditional melodies. During the chanting of the seven wedding blessings, the bride and groom were covered with a prayer shawl. Receptions would be more or less lavish, depending on the family's financial abilities.

During the week following the wedding, the bride's trousseau (*ashugar*) was displayed for guests. The trousseau was a source of pride and honor for the bride and her family, and mothers would begin sewing and crocheting for the trousseau when their daughters were still quite young. The week after the wedding was characterized by daily visits and celebrations among family and friends.

On the Sabbath following the wedding, the groom took a special Torah scroll from the ark, aside from the scroll used for the weekly Torah reading. After the regular Torah reading was completed, the groom brought his Torah scroll to the reader's desk, amidst the singing of the congregation. The portion of Genesis 24:1–7 was chanted, describing when Abraham commanded his servant to find a wife for Isaac. The *hazzan* chanted each verse in Hebrew, and then another individual sang the traditional Aramaic translation. Each verse was sung to a different melody. This ceremony was known as the *Avraham siv*, derived from the first two words of the Aramaic translation of Genesis 24:1. Following synagogue services, congregants escorted the newlyweds to their home, where a light repast was served. Refreshments included Jordan almonds (*novyas*), baklava, and candies made of almond paste.

Death and Mourning Rituals

As a general rule, only men walked in a funeral procession and participated in burying the dead. Women mourners did not go to the cemetery until at least a month after a funeral. Based on kabbalistic teaching, sons did not go to the cemetery for the burial of their father.

The Jewish laws of mourning were observed as recorded in the *Shulhan Arukh*. Mourners sat on cushions on the floor during the seven days of mourning (known as the *siete*). Meals were prepared for them and their visitors by relatives and friends. Those who planned to visit mourners around mealtime would send food in advance, so as to avoid causing unnecessary trouble and expense to those preparing the meals.

Although public signs of mourning are normally forbidden on the Sabbath, some communities had the custom of having mourners sit in a specially designated section of the synagogue when they attended Sabbath services. Toward the end of services, congregants would move into the sections near the mourners, as a sign of consolation and communal solidarity. At the conclusion of synagogue services, people accompanied the mourners to their homes, where they read psalms for some time, before returning to their own homes for the Sabbath meal.

Mourners recited the *Kaddish* prayer until one week before the anniversary of the death of the one for whom they were mourning. It was customary for a mourner to purchase the honor of reading the haftarah on the Sabbath before the death anniversary date, a practice that continued in future years as well.

The anniversary of the death of a loved one was commemorated each year. Mourners recited *Kaddish* on the Shabbat before the anniversary date (or on Shabbat itself if the anniversary fell on Shabbat) and every day up to and including the anniversary date. The anniversary date, known among Ashkenazim as *yahrzeit*, was referred to by Sephardim as the *meldado* (reading, study session).

The *meldado* was commemorated on the evening of the death anniversary, at the home of one of the deceased's children or other relatives. Family members and friends were invited, with men sitting in one room and the women in another. Afternoon and evening services were chanted, after which the men would read selections from the Mishnah in memory of the one for whom the *meldado* was being observed. The rabbi delivered a talk, after which the hostess and other women passed around plates of food for the participants. The traditional fare for a *meldado* included sweet rolls, *biscochos* (baked sweet cookies), raisins, hard-boiled eggs (a traditional symbol of mourning), and Greek olives. Whiskey and raki, an anise-flavored liquor, were also served. Afterward, sweet pastries, halvah, and Turkish coffee would be passed around to the guests. The doors of the house were left open so that anyone could come in. Packages of food were prepared for guests, especially for the poor. These gatherings often lasted late into the night.

Professor Mair Jose Benardete considered the *meldado* to be a significant factor in maintaining Judeo-Spanish language and culture:

At the gatherings held for commemorating the dead, the Spanish used was that of everyday conversation. It was expected of the rabbi to give an edifying talk based on Jewish lore. By the time he began his discourse in an informal manner, the women and children in the house would approach the open door of the room where the lighted candles on the paisley shawl glowed, and the men who had said the evening prayers were ready to listen to the stories prepared by the rabbi for the occasion.... By the time the rabbi finished with his stories, all had relaxed, their troubles were forgotten, and their feeling of solidarity through religious practice and language participation was strengthened.[20]

In close-knit communities, where nearly everyone was related by blood or marriage, life-cycle events brought families together on a regular basis. On any given week, someone in the family was celebrating a birth, circumcision, engagement, marriage, or *meldado*. These events served as a bedrock of social life, family and communal solidarity, and religious traditionalism.

Sabbaths, Festivals, and Holy Days

A dominant theme of the Sabbath, festival, and holy day observances was joy. *Hemdat ha-Yamim*, in discussing the laws and customs of Rosh Hashanah, expressed an idea that was common to all the holy days:

> When one leaves from the synagogue [after prayer services] he should go home and rejoice his heart and gladden his honor [i.e., soul] and trust in Blessed God, and chant the kiddush with full heart and willing soul. He should distance from himself sadness and sighs, so as not to give an opening to the "prosecutor" [angel], who only can find his way in [to our lives] where there is sadness and sighs and discord and argument.... One must rejoice in his heart and

show happiness to all, in order to blind the eye of the Satan. He should set his table and eat and rejoice since it is a holy day.... We were not commanded to be silly and foolish but to have the happiness of the mitzvah. One should gladden the hearts of the poor, the orphans and the widows.... It is not proper to eat and drink overly much, but rather less than a full amount, so that one does not become light-headed due to overeating.[21]

Even during the High Holy Day season, when the theme was penitence for one's sins, Sephardim maintained a spirit of joy. In 1774, an Ashkenazic rabbi, Simha ben Yehoshua, was on a ship traveling to the Land of Israel on a pilgrimage. Most of the Jews on board were Sephardim. The voyage took place during Elul, the month of repentance preceding Rosh Hashanah. Rabbi Simha made the following observation:

On the entire voyage, we prayed with the Sephardim. The Sephardim awoke prior to daybreak to say the penitential prayers with a quorum, as is their custom during the month of Elul. During the day, they eat and rejoice and are happy of heart. Some of them spend their entire days in study.[22]

The synagogue services on Rosh Hashanah and Yom Kippur were chanted in an uplifting tone. Certainly, the music reflected the seriousness of these holy days—the time when each human being stands in judgment before God. Yet, the music of the services was not tearful or overly somber. Indeed, many of the prayers chanted by the congregation actually sounded happy. One of the solemn hymns sung on Yom Kippur, for example, has the following refrain: *hatanu l'fanekha rahem aleinu,* "we have sinned before You, have mercy on us." This hymn was sung with great enthusiasm to a lively melody. If one did not know what the words meant, one would think the Sephardim were singing a happy song—not a con-trite confession of sinfulness.

The Sephardic spirit was essentially optimistic and happy. Yes, they recited penitential prayers and confessed their sins. But they maintained a confident belief that God loved them, was compassionate, wanted them to rejoice in God's blessings. This attitude, evident even on the most solemn days of the Jewish calendar, characterized the Sephardim throughout the year.

Rabbi Eliyahu ha-Cohen, an eighteenth-century sage of Izmir, explained a Talmudic passage that lauds two jokesters who were said to have been granted eternal reward in the world-to-come.

> Anyone who is happy all his days thereby indicates the greatness of his trust in God. That is why they [the jokesters] were always happy. Even when evil befell them, they knew that their sins had brought this on and were happy that these sufferings were for their own good, to purify them. This quality [of accepting life with happiness] is enough to give a person merit to have a place in the world-to-come; for great is trust [in God], even if a person is not perfect in all other moral perfections.[23]

For the Jews, the Sabbaths and holy days were wonderful respites from the challenges and difficulties of daily life. Rich or poor, each Jew celebrated these days with happiness, family and communal fellowship, and special meals. They wore their best clothes and ate the best food they could afford. One of the popular Shabbat hymns sung by the Jews of Turkey at their Sabbath meals begins, *Miyom rishon ad yom shishi, likrat Shabbat nikhsefah nafshi, ki be-Shabbat etsei hofshi, vekhi yom m'nuhah ekra'ehu,* "From Sunday to Friday, my soul longs to greet the Sabbath; because on the Sabbath I go free, and I call it a day of tranquility." The Sabbath and festival rituals provided a warm, traditional framework for celebrating and for feeling free.

While the Sephardim observed these days with culinary specialties they had brought with them from Spain, they soon introduced many foods typical of the Turkish cuisine as well.[24]

Shabbat and holidays each had their special foods, prepared by the women of the household. In the days before refrigeration, home ovens, and electric appliances, the women worked laboriously to prepare the festive meals. They used fresh ingredients (e.g., spinach, leek, okra, squash, potatoes, eggplant, as well as chicken and meat) and had to clean, peel, and chop everything by hand. They used little outdoor ovens or grills to cook the food, or they brought their things to be baked in communal ovens.

A Friday night meal might include *pescado con tomat* (fish in a tomato/lemon sauce) or *pescado con huevo y limon* (fish in avgolemono sauce), followed by a main course of chicken, *macaron enreinado* (a pasta dish baked with chopped meat and parsley), stuffed vegetables, *fasoulias* (string beans cooked in an oil sauce), *barbounias* (shell beans, cooked in a tomato sauce), potatoes, or other vegetable dishes. The meal might also include *pastelicos* (triangular or round pastries, filled with a mixture of chopped meat, eggs, onions, and vegetables) and *yaprakes* (grape leaves stuffed with a rice or meat filling). For dessert, fresh fruit and roasted nuts would be served, along with homemade sweets including halvah, baklava, kadayif, tispishti, and loukoum.

On Shabbat morning, synagogue services were generally held early and were concluded by 9:00 or 9:30 a.m. Families would then have their morning meal, *desayuno*, which would feature dairy foods. Most popular were *bourekas* (pastry or filo dough, filled with mixtures of potato, cheese, spinach, or eggplant), *boulemas* (an oily-doughed pastry filled with spinach or eggplant and cheese), *huevos haminados* (hard-boiled eggs, cooked overnight in water, onionskins, and a bit of oil, so that the eggshells turned brown), *frittata* (quiche-type casseroles made of spinach and cheese or shredded zucchini and cheese mixture), *rosca* (a round baked pastry, filled with jam and topped with sesame seeds), fresh fruit, and melons. The women would also prepare a large quantity of baked goods that served as bread for the meals, as well as snacks for during the day: sweet rolls, *panderas* (breads), *pandaricas* (pretzel-shaped snacks made of bread dough, baked until crisp), *biscochos* (crispy, sweet round snacks, topped with sesame seeds), and *pepitas* (toasted sunflower or pumpkin seeds).

Following the morning meal, families would have some quiet time, and then the rest of the afternoon was given to visiting with family, friends, and neighbors. Study sessions for children and adults took place at the synagogue during the course of the afternoon. After the afternoon prayer was recited, the men and children returned home for the third Sabbath meal. Then they would again return to the synagogue for the evening prayers and the *Havdalah* service that separated the holiness of the Sabbath from the mundane workdays. Under the influence of the kabbalists of Safed, many Sephardim had a festive meal (*m'laveh malkah*) after the Sabbath had concluded, as a way of escorting out the Sabbath queen.

The Sephardim of the Ottoman Empire cannot be understood without reference to their rich religious traditions, family life, and communal solidarity. The Sabbaths, festivals, and holy days were essential ingredients in their lives, providing them not only with spiritual sustenance but with tangible material and social pleasures. However problematic their economic and political situations may have been, their inner lives were filled with faith, pride, joy, and a strong sense of belonging to a special people.[25]

Ladino Folklore

Professor Mair Jose Benardete believed that "culturally speaking, the linguistic triumph of the Castilian tongue was the most significant happening that occurred in the transplanted Hispanic world."[1] The Jewish exiles from fifteenth-century Spain brought their Hispanic culture and character to their new homes in the Ottoman Empire and absorbed the indigenous Jews into the Sephardic mold.

The various Sephardic communities had their own linguistic characteristics—pronunciation, word usage, borrowings from other languages. Yet, the language was universally understood among them and was a strong unifying force. It can be stated fairly that the Judeo-Spanish-speaking Sephardim of the Ottoman Empire formed a distinctive civilization with a basic unity of culture.[2] They shared a common worldview, a rich literature in both Hebrew and Ladino, and a vibrant folklore tradition.

Religious Songs in Ladino

Sephardim expressed their deepest emotions in their vernacular language. Ladino was the language of their minds and hearts; it was the vehicle of their civilization and way of life. Their language separated them from the non-Jewish society that surrounded them, as well as from the non-Judeo-Spanish-speaking Jewish communities of the world. It was, thus, distinctively theirs; it linked them to each other and evoked memories of the earlier generations who also spoke this language.

Ladino, along with Hebrew, was part of the religious culture of the Sephardim. Ladino translations of Hebrew hymns and prayers were incorporated into the synagogue services. The rabbi's sermon was delivered in Judeo-Spanish. Ladino hymns were sung at the Shabbat meals, as well as at the *Havdalah* ceremony at the conclusion of the Sabbath. A popular Hebrew song sung at the Shabbat table was *Yom ha-Shabbat Ein Kamohu* ("There Is No Day Like the Sabbath Day"). The first stanzas praise the beauty and sanctity of the Sabbath. The last stanza, though, focuses on the uniqueness of the people of Israel. Interestingly, it was customary in many homes to sing the last stanza in Ladino translation as a way of underscoring this message: *Envelunto A-donai y escojo en nos, y mas que todo lashon nos aparto, y santeficamiento de el Shabbat nos hizo heredar todo semen de Yaacov, lo honramos a el dia del Shabbat, no hay como el, no hay como el, lo bendicho el Dio y lo santefico.* (The Lord wished and chose us, and set us apart from all nations; and the holiness of Shabbat the Lord gave as an inheritance to all of us of the seed of Jacob. We honor the Sabbath day; there is none like it, there is none like it. God blessed and sanctified it.)

A widespread custom, going into the twentieth century (and still practiced in a number of congregations today), was the singing of Ladino-translated *selihot,* penitential hymns sung at early morning services during the month of Elul. On Rosh Hashanah and Yom Kippur, a number of lilting hymns were sung by the congregation in Ladino translation. On Shavuot, the *ketubah de la ley* was chanted; it was a poetic piece celebrating the "marriage" of the people of Israel to the Torah. On the fast day of the ninth of Av, Hebrew dirges were sung in Ladino translation.

A genre of poetry/songs developed as *coplas de Purim,* humorous pieces sung on the occasion of the happy holiday of Purim. In most Sephardic homes, the Passover Haggadah was chanted in both Hebrew and Ladino, and Ladino translations of Pesah songs such as *Had Gadya* and "Who Knows One?" were sung at the conclusion of each Seder. During the weeks between Pesah and Shavuot, *Pirkei Avot* (*Ethics of the Fathers*) was chanted in Ladino on Shabbat afternoons.

Following the recitation of the Grace after Meals in Hebrew, it was the practice in some Sephardic communities to chant a short grace in Ladino. This was ostensibly for the benefit of women and children who did not know Hebrew; in fact, it also was beneficial to many men, whose comprehension of Hebrew was insufficient to grasp the meaning of the words of the Hebrew Grace. This prayer demonstrates the interspersing of Hebrew words into Ladino texts. It also follows the Ladino practice of referring to God as *Dio* rather than the Castilian *Dios*, since the Castilian word ends with the letter "s"—normally a sign of a plural word. The text of the Ladino Grace is:

> *Ya comimos y bevimos, y al Dio santo Barukh Hu uvarukh Shemo bendishimos; que mos dio y mos dara pan para comer y panyos para vestir y anyos para bivir. El Padre el grande que mande al chico asegun tenemos de menester para muestras casas y para muestros hijos. El Dio mos oiga y mos aresponda y mos apiade por su nombre el grande, que somos almicas sin pecado. Hodu l'Adonai ki tov ki le-olam hasdo. Hodu l'Adonai ki tov ki le-olam hasdo. Siempre mejor, nunca peor, nunca mos manke la meza del Criador, Amen.* (We have eaten and drunk, and we bless the Holy One blessed be He and His holy Name; who has given us and gives us bread to eat, and clothes to wear and years to live. The Almighty Father who provides for the littlest one—so may He provide that we have the necessities for our homes and for our children. May God hear us and respond to us, and have pity on us for the sake of His great name; for we are little souls without sin. Praise the Lord for He is good, for His kindness is everlasting. Praise the Lord

for He is good, for His kindness is everlasting. May things always be better, never worse; may the Creator's table never be lacking for us, Amen.)

These Ladino religious songs enjoyed a special sanctity among the Sephardim. They were important not simply for their religious message, but because of the Ladino itself. They were sung with understanding and reverence. The Sephardic sages, who translated and introduced Ladino pieces into the synagogue liturgy, were far ahead of their time. It was not until the modern period that European and American congregations introduced readings in the vernacular into their synagogue services, and in many cases, these vernacular readings were opposed by traditionalists, who viewed them as "reforms." Yet, for the Sephardim, prayers in the vernacular—both in the synagogue and at home—were a vital and traditional component of their religious lives for centuries.

Romances

Over the centuries, Sephardim maintained a rich tradition of songs in Ladino. A genre known as *romances* included ballads and songs of love and other emotions. Professor David Romey, in his study of the Ladino traditions of the Sephardim in Seattle, described the singing of *romances*:

On many occasions of festive gatherings, the *romances* are sung in chorus, that is, everyone who knows or can follow the words and the music sings. The effect is very pleasing and lends itself to more singing, until someone with a good voice takes a solo and the rest come in on the choral tag-phrase. The theme of the *romances* sung at these parties is usually the lyric love theme far removed from the solemnity of epic material. *Romances* are never interspersed with other types of song. Somehow one suggests another in a chain-reaction effect. But whether or not there be any special occasion, one is never really in need of a reason to sing a *romance*.[3]

Although some Ladino songs had biblical or other religious themes, the vast majority related to general human experience: love, death, jealousy, marriage, and such. Not a few of the songs were brought by the Sephardim from Spain.[4] That Sephardic Jews continued to sing medieval Spanish love songs and ballads for centuries—while living in isolation from Spain or any other Spanish-speaking country—was a phenomenon of remarkable historical and cultural significance. Sephardim sang these songs quite naturally and were not self-conscious about their amazing accomplishment in maintaining medieval Spanish musical and linguistic traditions. When Spanish scholars "discovered" the Sephardim in the early twentieth century, they were astounded to find medieval Spanish traditions still living and thriving among them.

In the summer of 1903, the Spanish senator Angel Pulido met some Sephardic Jews aboard a ship on which they were all traveling. He was astonished to hear them speaking in an archaic-sounding Spanish language. He struck up a friendship with a Sephardic fellow passenger, Dr. Enrique Bejerano, director of the Sephardic school in Bucharest. Bejerano was an erudite, cultured scholar, conversant in a number of languages. Pulido was profoundly moved by his meeting with Bejerano, and he excitedly reported back to his colleagues in Spain that he had come into contact with Sephardic Jews who still spoke medieval Spanish. Pulido wrote a book *Españoles sin patria (Spaniards Without a Country)*, published in Madrid in 1905, which included his correspondence with Sephardic intellectuals and communal leaders throughout the Judeo-Spanish-speaking world—Turkey, Greece, the Balkans, Morocco, Israel, South America, and the United States.

Pulido viewed the Sephardim as a treasure of Spanish history and culture, who had maintained their Hispanic culture in spite of their having been expelled from Spain in 1492. He praised

Sephardic scholars and researchers—including Abraham Danon, Abraham Galante, and Jose Benoliel—who were busily collecting and publishing Ladino folklore, thereby preserving medieval Spanish traditions. Pulido's enthusiasm quickly spread among Spanish scholars, resulting in much research relating to Sephardic history and culture.

It is important to note, though, that the Sephardim themselves did not sing *romances* with the aim of maintaining medieval Spanish cultural traditions. Rather, they sang these songs as organic and pleasurable aspects of their own lives, not as relics of a distant past.

While many songs could indeed be traced back to Spain, many others were composed by Sephardim after the expulsion from Spain. The *romance* tradition was alive; it grew and developed over the generations; new songs were composed in the spirit and style of the old. In short, these songs played a singular role in the everyday life of the Judeo-Spanish-speaking Sephardim.

Professor David Romey has suggested that the majority of the melodies of the *romances* were of Peninsular origin. Although Sephardim in Turkey learned Turkish music and enjoyed Turkish melodies and dances, the traditional Ladino songs had a distinctive Spanish/Moorish flavor.

> *Romance* tunes and Turkish tunes are distinct in this respect, that both are kept separate like two albums on a shelf. Turkish tunes are reserved primarily for the dance. I have never seen or heard of a dance associated with a *romance*. Nor have I heard anyone speak of a new tune for a *romance*, although there are a few variations of the same basic melody.[5]

Since Ladino songs were generally sung in groups, rather than performed by soloists for an audience, they engaged members of the group as active participants rather than as passive listeners. Thus, people more naturally learned the words and tunes of the songs, since they themselves were among the singers. Ladino singing was a group happening, a mode of entertainment for families, friends, and neighbors. Although men also sang Ladino songs, the women were the main bearers of the *romance* tradition. Women sang together when they cooked, when they prepared for family celebrations, when they needed a respite from their daily routines. They also sang Ladino lullabies to their children.

Although there were religious pietists who objected to singing love songs, the *romances* were very popular throughout all strata of Sephardic society. Men and women often sang these songs together. It was not unusual for women to sing solo parts in the presence of men. People participated in the singing and enjoyed the songs in a natural, easygoing way.[6]

Pious Jews and Jewesses did not blush while singing songs of passionate love, even songs that reflected immoral behavior. One of the popular songs, *El Rey Por Muncha Madruga*, tells of a king who came into his queen's room while she was combing her hair early one morning.[7] She had been expecting her lover and did not realize it was the king who had entered her room. Thinking she was talking to her lover she proceeded to recount that she had two sons by the king and two by the lover, and that she treated the latter's sons much better than the king's. After making this fatal admission, she turned around and saw the king. She quickly made up an excuse that she had been having a strange dream. The king, though, was not fooled by her ruse and ordered her to be beheaded at daybreak. A variant of this song has the queen curse her lover before she is beheaded. She warns: Woe unto women who trust men.[8]

Another song describes the conversation between a mother and her daughter.[9] The daughter has a sprig of rue and a flower in her hand. The mother asks where she got them. The daughter replies that they were a gift from a young man who was in love with her. The mother warns her daughter not to lead a life of sin, that a bad husband (the daughter is apparently already married!) is better than a new lover. The daughter, though, maintains her devotion to the lover. The mother pleads that the daughter not let herself fall into sin.

The following selection of *romances* reflects a range of powerful emotions, expressed in fine poetic language.

La rosa enflorece en el mes de mayo,	The rose blooms in the month of May,
Mi alma se espulece pensando en tu amor.	My soul blossoms thinking of your love.
Las noches son fortunas los dias son males,	The nights are fortunate, the days are bad,
El amor y mi ventura esta en tu poder.	Love and my future are in your power.
Mas presto ven palomba, mas presto salvame.	Come more quickly my dove, more quickly save me.
El amor y me ventura esta en tu poder.	Love and my future are in your power.
El bilbilico canta en arvoles de flor,	The nightingale sings in the flowering trees,
Alli debaxo se asentan los que sufren del amor.[10]	There beneath sit those who suffer from love.

⁓

Arvoles lloran por luvia	Trees cry for rain
Y montanas por aire.	And mountains for wind.
Ansi lloran los mis ojos	So do my eyes cry
Por ti querida amante.	For you, dear lover.
En frente de mi hay un angelo	In front of me is an angel
Con sus ojos me mira.	Who looks at me with his eyes.
Havlar quero y non puedo,	I wish to speak but cannot,
Mi corason suspire.	My heart heaves.
Ven veras, y ven veras,	Come see, and come see,
Y ven veras, veremos.	Come see, and we shall see,
Amor que tenemos los dos,	The love that we two share,
Ven mos aunaremos.[11]	Come let us be united.

Todos se van a la quehila,
Yo vengo a tu casa,
Estrellica la mi alma.
Todos besan la mezuzah,
Yo beso tus caras,
Estrellica la mi alma.
—Tu madre se hue al bedahe
A rogar que me muera,
Por no tomar esta nuera.

Tu madre se hue al bedahe,
Y tambien tus hermanas,
Por no tomar esta cunada.[12]

Everyone goes to the synagogue,
I come to your house,
Little Estrella, my soul.
Everyone kisses the mezuzah,
I kiss your cheeks,
Little Estrella, my soul.
—Your mother went to the cemetery
To pray for my death,
To avoid having me as her
    daughter-in-law.

Your mother went to the cemetery,
And your sisters too,
So as not to have me as a sister-
    in-law.

La mancevez yo la pedri
Por tu amor querida,
Ahinda yo no encontri
Cura a mi ferida.
Cuando nos vamos encontrar
Al mundo verdadero,

A ti te van a preguntar
Por tu amor primero.
Y si el Dio te juzgara
Te topara culposa,
Ma yo mismo me acusare
Por ti mi linda rosa.[13]

I have lost my youth
For your love, dear,
But I have not yet found
A cure to my wound.
When we encounter
The true world [i.e., the world-to-
    come],

They will ask you
About your first love.
And if God will judge you
He will find you guilty,
But I myself will take the guilt
For you my pretty rose.

Bien sabe la rosa	The rose knows well
En que mano posa;	In whose hand she rests;
El mancebo loco	The young man is delirious
En moza hermosa.	Over the beautiful maiden.
Dama, ansi es deber,	So, my lady, it is necessary,
Dama, ansi es razon,	So, my lady, it is fitting,
Que salgais a bailar	That you go out to dance
Que vos quiero ver.	For I wish to see you.
Si mi sinor m'olvido	If I should forget my father
Yo nunca la olvidare.[14]	Yet never shall I forget you.

Como la rosa en la guerta	As a rose in the garden
Y las flores sin avrir,	Whose blossoms have not yet opened,
Ansi es una donzella	So is a maiden
A las horas del murir.	In the hours of her death.
Tristes horas en el dia	They were sad hours in the day
Que hazina ya cayo,	When she fell ill,
Como la reina en su lecho	As a queen in her bed
Ya cayo y se dezmayo.	She fell and fainted.
Lagrimas de una madre	Tears of a mother,
El Dio y alas va sinter.	God will hear them.
Pensa que agora nacites,	Think that you were born now,
Espera buen avenir.	Hope for a good future.
Su gracia y su mirada	Her charm and beauty
Era mi consolacion:	Have been my consolation:
Al mi lado se asentava	She has sat by my side,
Su mano en mi corason.	Her hand on my heart.
Avrid puertas y ventanas	Open the doors and windows
A mi hija acudir;	To save my daughter;
Quen la via la llorava	Whoever sees her weeps
De ver este angel murir.[15]	To watch this angel die.

Maldicha es la mi vida
Siempre sufro con dolor,
De ver lejos de mi,
A mi angel mi amor.
Desgraciado so en el mundo
Sin ver mas la tu color,
La tierra ya te cobija—
Que mancilla y que dolor.
En tu blanca fresca tomba
Mis males te vo contra.
Cada dia en tu tomba
Una flor te v'a plantar.[16]

Cursed is my life
I always suffer with sorrow,
To see you far from me,
My angel, my love.
Unfortunate am I in the world
No longer able to see your color,
The earth covers you—
What a tragedy, what sadness.
On your fresh tomb
I will recount my woes.
Each day on your tomb
I will plant a flower.

Secretos quero descubrir,
Secretos de mi vida,
No lo sabeis mis hermanos
Ni primos ni parientes.
Los cielos quero por papel,
La mar quero por tinta,
Los arboles por pendolas
Para escribir mis dertes.
Cerra a la puerta t'hablare,
Sale a la ventana,
Te hablare, te descubrire
Secretos de mi alma.
Arbolico de yazemin
En mi huerta plantado,
T'engrandeci, t'enfloreci,

Otro s'esta gozando.[17]

I wish to reveal secrets,
Secrets of my life,
My brothers don't know them
Nor my cousins and relatives.
I need the sky for paper,
I need the sea for ink,
The trees for pens
To write my sorrows.
Close the door and I will tell you,
Move from the window,
I will tell you, I will reveal to you
The secrets of my soul.
A little jasmine bush
I planted in my garden,
I tended you, I helped you
    flourish,
Another enjoyed you.

Like the *romance El Rey Por Muncha Madruga* described above, many *romances* clearly harked back to the legends of medieval Spain, and dealt with kings and queens, knights, and other noteworthy characters. Professor Max Grunwald's (1871–1953) collection of songs from Sephardic Jews in Vienna includes such titles as "The Sinful Queen," who betrays her husband by taking a lover; "Dovergile," who falls in love with the king's niece; "The Daughter of the Cid," who marries the king; "Why Do You Cry, Fair Maiden?", which deals with a seafaring knight; "My Father Comes from Brusa, My Mother from Aragon," which tells of a woman whose husband abandons her, but then returns as a knight; "The Moorish King's Daughter," who is sought in marriage by a knight; "Gimina," who demands of the king of Leon that he and his nephew Diego avenge the death of her father; and "Don Buezo and His Sister," a love story involving the king of the Moors and the daughter of the Austrian king.[18]

The rich and expansive repertoire of Ladino songs reflects the Sephardic ability to be comfortable with the themes of love, grief, jealousy, and other profound emotions. The Sephardim saw no sharp conflict between the teachings of religion and the singing of *romances*; emotions were part of the human experience and therefore were appropriate themes for songs.

The *romances* kept the Sephardic imagination and sense of beauty alive and active. Through these songs, shoemakers and street-porters, merchants and barbers, housewives and grandmothers were able to rise above the tedium of their daily drudgery. Their songs did not bewail their poverty or make them feel sorry for their economic and political shortcomings. Rather, the music reached outward, opening broad vistas and stimulating deep feelings. These songs were expressions of poetry and poetic imagery, well-chosen words set to lilting melodies. Sephardim—no matter how poor—sang of the power of love; the beauties of nature; the deeds of kings, queens, and knights.

Ladino songs reflected and influenced the Sephardic appreciation of graceful behavior and good manners. Various songs describe the proper and dignified customs that exist among parents and children, the parents of brides and grooms, and husbands and wives. Indeed, the *romances* form a remarkable literary corpus that reflects important aspects of the inner life of Sephardim: sensitivity, grace, honor, dignity, openness to emotions, poetry, imagination.[19]

Proverbs and Folk Sayings

The commonsense folk wisdom of the people found expression in numerous Ladino proverbs and sayings. Many of them derived from biblical and rabbinic sources. Others had Spanish origins. Yet others were Ladino translations of proverbs in Turkish, French, and other languages with which the Sephardim had familiarity. Proverbs could be applied to almost any personality or situation and often contained elements of satire and humor.

Collections of traditional Ladino proverbs and sayings have been compiled and published by scholars and laymen alike. While almost all of them were based on the traditions of Sephardim who lived during the late nineteenth and early twentieth centuries, it can be assumed that most of these proverbs went back to earlier periods. Folk sayings are naturally transmitted from one generation to the next.

Although the collected Ladino proverbs are diverse—and sometimes offer contradictory messages—it is possible to detect major themes that reflect general folk attitudes of Sephardim.[20] The following proverbs underscore the belief that a person should not be judged on the basis of external factors. Wealth and power do not make one better than others.

> *El rey es con la gente.* (The king is with the people: One should not be aloof and snobby, thinking oneself superior to others. True nobility means identifying with all the people.)
>
> *Los ojos no se inchen con moneda sino con polvo de tierra.* (At the time of death, the eyes are not filled with money, but with the dust of the earth: A person should not attribute excessive

importance to wealth, but should rather concentrate on being a virtuous person. When one stands in judgment before God in the world-to-come, he or she will not be able to bring his or her money, but only his or her good deeds. Everyone—rich or poor—meets the same fate: death.)

El diamente briya, pero al fin y al cavo es piedra. (The diamond glitters, but in the final analysis it is just a rock: even if a person glitters with wealth, in the final analysis he or she is only flesh and blood—no better than anyone else.)

Prove de moneda no es prove, prove de ideas es prove. (Poverty of money is not poor; poverty of ideas is poor.)

Un dia en la silla del rey es un dia. (One day on the throne of a king is one day: all mortals are essentially the same, subject to the same destiny.)

Kada uno saluda kon el chapeyo ke tyene. (Everyone salutes with the hat he has: whether rich or poor, each person confronts life with what he or she has.)

La muerte no konose ni riko ni prove. (Death does not know the difference between rich and poor.)

The following proverbs relate to the role of friends and neighbors. Since people are much influenced by their friends and neighbors, one must try to associate with good people.

El Dio que te guadre de vezino malo. (May God protect you from a bad neighbor.)

El Dio adelantre y el vezino despues. (First God and then a neighbor: When one needs assistance, one should first pray to God; but then, one must turn to a neighbor who is readily available to provide aid. Therefore, one should be sure to have a good neighbor.)

Mejor solo que mal acompanado. (It is better to be alone than to be badly accompanied.)

Del Dio y del vezino nada no se encubri. (From God and from a neighbor nothing is hidden.)

No con quien naces sino con quien paces. (It is not among whom
you were born, but among whom you live: a person's character is not determined by birth, but is much influenced by
the society in which one lives.)

The following proverbs refer to family relationships.

Hermano para el dia malo. (A brother for a bad day: when one
is in trouble, it is one's brother who will come to the rescue,
i.e., blood is thicker than water.)

No hay amigo en el mundo mas que la madre. (There is no friend
in the world greater than one's mother.)

Suegra ni de barro buena. (A mother-in-law, even if she were
made of clay, is no good.)

Quien te ama mas de mama, de palavras te engania. (One who says
he loves you more than your mother [loves you] is deceiv-
ing you with his words.)

Una madre i una manta tapan munchas faltas. (A mother and a
blanket can cover many faults [defects].)

Hijos de mis hijos, dos vezes mis hijos. (The children of my children are doubly my children: the love of grandparents for
their grandchildren.)

A number of Ladino proverbs reflect on Jewish attitudes
toward Jews and non-Jews.

Gudio bovo no hay. (There is no stupid Jew.)

El gudio kuando kevra si asavienta. (When a Jew errs, he learns
from his mistake.)

Kual banker sino el gudio? (Who is a banker [i.e., has good business sense] if not a Jew?)

Gudio ki no ayuda a otro non ay. (There is no Jew who does not
help another.)

El gudio savi lo ke otros no tienin ni la idea. (The Jew knows what
others don't even have an idea about.)

Si el gudio es torpe, guay del Turko. (If the Jew is stupid, woe unto the Turk.)

El gudio bive riko, muere prove. El grego bive prove, muere riko. (The Jew lives rich and dies poor. The Greek lives poor and dies rich.)

Ya se izo judio. (He has become a Jew, i.e., one has matured, become intelligent.)

El turko dimanda sedaka en kantando, el grego yorando, el gudio en malkiziendo. (The Turk begs for charity while singing, the Greek while crying, the Jew while cursing.)

De adientro de una carpuz salio un judio. (From inside of a watermelon, out came a Jew!: Jews can be found everywhere, even where least expected.)

The following proverbs relate to the virtue of having compassion for the poor and downtrodden.

El harto no cree al hambriento. (One who is full does not believe one who is hungry: If one has an abundance of food, one may not fully understand the plight of the poor who lack adequate food. Not sympathizing with the pain of those who are hungry, one will not feel compelled to provide suitable assistance.)

Tanto lavora el provi k'el rico si enrikese. (The poor man works so hard that the rich man gets rich: the employees do the hard work, while the wealthy owners receive most of the profits.)

En dia de luvia pensa en el provi; el tambien tiene frio. (On a rainy day, think of the poor; they also are cold.)

Some proverbs deal with matters relating to economics.

Ken bivi kon ispiranza bivi alegri ma si mueri di ambri. (One who lives with hope [alone] lives happily, but will die of hunger.)

Quien merca lo que no tiene de menester, vende lo que tiene de menester. (One who buys something that he does not need will

come to sell that which he does need: spending money friv-
olously can lead to poverty.)

De lo barato se povrecio mi padre. (From buying inexpensive
things, my father became impoverished.)

El que tiene quatro y gasta cinco, no tiene menester de bolsa. (One
who has four and spends five has no need for a pocket: do
not spend more than you have.)

Dingun lavoro no te dezenora, ma te proveca i te onora. (No work
dishonors you, but it raises you and honors you: gainful
employment is worthy, even in menial occupations.)

Vende pipinos vende halva, i no asperes a nedavah. (Sell cucum-
bers, sell halvah, but don't expect anything from charity.)

Vende pepitas, vende kalavasa i detente de onor en plasa. (Sell
pumpkin seeds, sell squash, but maintain your honor.)

Ken mira la gente nunka bive kontente. (Who looks at the people
[i.e., what other people have or do] never lives with con-
tentment: one who is always concerned to keep up with
others and to maintain false appearances will not be
happy.)

The following proverbs deal with adversity.

En el mal se konosen los baraganes. (Through suffering can one
recognize strong men: a person's strength of character is
demonstrated by how he or she copes with misfortune.)

No ay mal ke no seya para byen. (There is no misfortune that is
not for the good.)

Si los anillos cayeron, los dedos quedaron. (If the rings fell off, the
fingers remained: even if you lost something of impor-
tance, you still have retained the main thing.)

El amojado no se espanta de la luvia. (The one who is wet is not
afraid of the rain: A person who has already passed through
a difficult situation does not fear further challenges, since he
or she is experienced in facing the problems. One is already
"wet" and has nothing to lose by being in the "rain.")

Quien es el ciego? El que no quere ver. (Who is blind? One who does not wish to see: if one does not want to face the facts, one will face adversity through his or her own blindness of insight.)

Si tu enemigo es una hormiga contalo como un gamello. (If your enemy is an ant, consider him to be a camel: Do not underestimate the damage that can be done to you even by an insignificant enemy. If you overestimate your enemy's power, you will be better able to defend yourself from his or her malice.)

Ande va la piedra, en el ojo de la ciega. (Where does the rock go but into the eye of a blind person: trouble strikes a person who already has trouble.)

The following proverbs offer general wisdom on coping with life.

Todos los dedos de la mano no son unos. (All the fingers of the hand are not the same: diversity is part of life; everyone is different.)

Pasa punto, pasa mundo. (A moment passes, a world passes.)

Hablad la verdad, perded la amistad. (Speak the truth and lose friendship: One cannot always be blunt with others by pointing out the "truth" to them, since this may antagonize them. A diplomatic approach is more effective.)

Azno cayado por savio es tomado. (A silent donkey is taken to be a sage: the virtue of silence.)

En boka serada no entra moshka. (Into a closed mouth, a fly does not enter: if you don't talk too much, you will avoid trouble.)

El ke pensa muncho no se va a Yerushalayim. (One who thinks [overly] much will not go to Jerusalem: one who is too reflective and too cautious will not take the risks necessary to achieve a great goal like going to Jerusalem.)

Mas vale rabino sin barva ke barva sin rabino. (A rabbi without a beard is better than a beard without a rabbi.)

El Dio es tadriozo ma no olvidozo. (God is slow but not forgetful.)

Lo ke El Dio kere, esto es. (That which God wants, that's what is.)

Cuando te llaman azno mira si tienes cola. (When they call you a jackass, look to see if you have a tail: Perhaps they are right! Conversely, if you have no "tail," you need not pay attention to their criticism.)

Va ande te llaman y no ande te queren. (Go where you are invited, not where you [think] you are wanted: wait for a formal invitation; do not assume you are welcome unless you are actually invited.)

Various proverbs comment on character traits.

De los ocho a los ochenta. (From eight to eighty: the character traits that one has at age eight remain throughout life.)

Quien azno nace, azno muere. (One who is born a donkey, dies a donkey: this is said of one who persists in his or her errors.)

Tanto dize amen basta que le caye el talet. (He says amen so much that his prayer shawl falls off: a critique of hypocritical behavior.)

Arrovan pitas y bezan mezuzot. (They steal bread and kiss mezuzot: they pretend to be pious but are in fact corrupt.)

No save apartar la calavasa de la berengena. (He doesn't know how to distinguish between a squash and an eggplant.)

Armado de bilibizes. (Armed with toasted garbanzos: this is said of a person who pretends to be strong and who bluffs others with his or her supposed power; yet, he or she has no real strength to back up his or her bluff.)

Arvole sin solombra. (A tree without shade: this is said of people who do not help others.)

Tu savis ma yo mas, diso el lonsu al haham. (You know but I know more, says the dullard to the sage.)

El haragan es kosejero. (The lazy one gives advice: it is ironic that the slothful person likes to advise others how to accomplish a task.)

Muncha miel bulanea. (Too much honey nauseates: excessive sweetness and self-righteousness are obnoxious.)

Despues de Purim platicos. (After Purim [he sends] plates: It is customary to send plates of sweets on Purim, as gifts to friends and neighbors. If one sends plates after Purim, i.e., does something tardily, one is subject to the criticism implied by this saying.)

The following proverbs relate to the virtue of self-reliance.

Poco ke sea, mio ke sea. (Let it be little, but let it be mine.)

A lo ke puedes solo no asperes de otros. (That which you can do alone, don't wait for others.)

Aremedyate kon lo tuyo, no seyas muhtach de dingunos. (Manage with what you have; don't be dependent on anyone.)

Gueso ke te kayo en parte, komelo kon arte. (Whatever bone falls to you, eat it gracefully: whatever your lot, make the best of it.)

Consejo de tu companero toma, y el de tu corason non dexes. (Take the advice of your companion, but do not abandon that of your own heart: receiving advice can be beneficial, but ultimately you must remain faithful to your own heart and make your own decision.)

Stories and Humor

Judeo-Spanish folk tradition is rich in stories. Stories were told to children, of course; but they were also told by adults to other adults as a form of entertainment. Many of them drew on biblical themes and rabbinic legends, while others told of more recent events and heroes. Some stories were grounded in tradition, and others were the product of the fancy of the storytellers.[21] Listeners derived a great deal of their pleasure not only from the story itself, but from the gestures and intonations of the storytellers. Even the blandest story could seem exciting or hilarious when properly related by a skilled narrator.

The general easygoing optimism manifested itself in the happy endings of many of the stories. Sephardic humor rarely reflected self-hatred or bitterness about being Jewish. The stories and humor tended to reinforce the notion that Jews were intelligent and compassionate, beloved by God.

By far the most popular figure in Sephardic storytelling and humor was Joha. This character was based on a Turkish folk personality Nasreddin Hodja, who was born in 1208. He was known to be a wise and witty character, famous for his comical antics. In some stories he cleverly outsmarts his antagonists, while in others he is depicted almost as an imbecile. It is said that before he died, he left instructions for a great door to be placed in front of his grave. The door was to be thick, solid, and heavily locked. But he also instructed that there should be no walls erected around his grave, so that a visitor to the tomb could simply walk around the huge locked door!

The word *hodja* is a Turkish word for "teacher," and refers specifically to a sage of religion. Since the original Hodja was a Muslim, the Jews re-created him by changing his name to Joha and dropping the Nasreddin. Thus, Joha carried no Muslim religious baggage and in fact was considered by many to be a Jewish character.

Joha's name became associated among Sephardim with odd and humorous behavior. Inappropriate, awkward actions were called *echas de Joha* (deeds of Joha). In order to deprecate an opinion, one simply said *ya avlo Joha* (Joha has spoken).

The following are examples of the tales of Joha that were popular among Sephardim for centuries.[22]

Joha and his wife were in need of money. They decided to sell their old, feeble donkey. Joha brought it to an auctioneer to sell in the marketplace. The auctioneer, in order to drum up business, sang out praises for the donkey: "Who will bid on this beautiful animal? It is young, strong, hardworking, with an excellent temperament." People began to bid for the donkey, and the price kept rising. All the while, the auctioneer continued to call out the marvelous qualities of the donkey. Joha was very impressed with the fine words of the auctioneer. But if the donkey was really so good, why should Joha allow it to fall into the hands of strangers? So Joha entered the bidding contest and finally succeeded in buying back his own donkey. How proud he was of his victory.

On one occasion, Joha went to the Turkish bath. The attendants treated him rudely, gave him an old towel, and hardly spoke to him. When he had finished at the bath, Joha gave each of the attendants a gold piece, a very generous tip. They were amazed by his generosity. The next time Joha came to the Turkish bath, the attendants treated him like a prince. They gave him the best towels, the best bath, the best massage. When he was ready to leave, Joha gave each of the attendants a tip of one small coin, worth practically nothing. The attendants were outraged. "How dare you give us such a small tip after we gave you such excellent service?" Joha replied, "Today's tip was for the previous time I came to the Turkish bath. The tip I gave you last time was to cover this visit."

One day, Joha's donkey ran away. Joha searched the entire city for it. He asked everyone he saw: "Have you seen my donkey?" Each person replied in the negative, to which Joha responded, "Praise the Lord." One man asked him, "Why do you praise the Lord because your donkey is lost?" Joha answered, "I praise the Lord that I was not riding on my donkey when he got lost. Otherwise, I too would be lost now."

One of Joha's neighbors asked to borrow his donkey. Joha replied, "Unfortunately, my donkey has died." At that very moment, though, the donkey brayed. The neighbor said, "Why do you lie to me? I just heard the voice of your donkey!" Joha replied solemnly, "What a skeptical person you are! Here I am, a man with a long white beard, and you don't believe me; yet you would believe the voice of a stupid donkey?"

One night, while Joha was sleeping, his wife pushed him and said, "Joha, will you please light the candle on your right?" Joha answered testily, "Are you out of your mind? In the midst of this darkness, is it possible for a person to know which way is right and which way is left?"

Joha was once walking down the street when he noticed something sparkling in a garbage heap. He rushed over and picked it up. It was a mirror. Upon looking into it, Joha said, "What an ugly picture! No wonder its owner threw it into the garbage heap."

A farmer gave Joha a duck as a present. To reciprocate for this kind gesture, Joha offered him a bowl of duck soup. A bit later, another man visited Joha, saying that he was a friend of the farmer who had given Joha the duck. Joha therefore also gave him a bowl of soup. Then a third man came and announced that he was a close friend of the farmer who had given Joha the duck. Joha served him a bowl of water. "But where is the duck soup?" the man protested. "I am a close friend of the farmer who gave you the duck." Joha replied, "Well, this water is a close friend of the duck soup!"

⌒

A poor, hungry man had only a piece of bread to eat. He passed by a restaurant and saw some meat frying in a pan over a fire. He placed his bread over the pan for a few seconds, hoping to absorb some of the flavor of the meat. The restaurant owner saw him and asked him to pay for the taste that he stole. The poor man could pay nothing, so the restaurant owner brought him to the judge, Joha, to demand his payment. Joha listened to the owner's claim and then took several coins out of his pocket. He asked the owner to listen carefully, and then Joha shook the coins so that they jingled. "What are you doing?" asked the owner. Joha replied, "I have just paid you for the damage caused to you by this poor man. The sound of the jingle of money is a fair price to pay for the odor of frying meat."

Superstitions

The Jews of the Ottoman Empire were much influenced by the prevailing beliefs and customs of the Muslim society. Jews, like their Muslim and Christian neighbors, believed in certain superstitions as well as in the efficacy of incantations, amulets, and other magical practices known among Jews as *s'gulot* (proven methods). Among the Sephardim, as among the non-Jewish communities, folk healing was widely practiced. The healers were often women, who learned their techniques from older women, generation to generation. Some rabbis also engaged in offering magical cures.[23] These beliefs and practices continued through the mid-twentieth century, although they declined significantly with the spread of western education and modern medicine.

Professor M. J. Benardete quoted at length from a Ladino memoir of Saadi Levy, a leading intellectual in Salonika during the late nineteenth and early twentieth centuries:

> Without any distinction of rank or age, all the inhabitants of Salonica, men and women, Jews and non-Jews, believed in the existence of evildoers [*sheddim*] who were also called "those who are better than we," or "those from below." Thousands of people swore that they had suffered the tricks and queer and ugly deeds of these phantoms; others affirmed having established their presence and heard their voices; still others went so far as to say they had seen and touched them. According to these weak minded people, the evil spirits assumed a thousand and one forms, of persons, of animals, of house objects, such as pieces of furniture, kitchen utensils, and other things. Often "those who are better than we" appeared as made partly of man, partly of animal, or partly of an object.... Whole families believed themselves assaulted by "those from below." They abandoned their houses and went to live in sections of the city far from their old abode without saying a word to anyone....[24]

What was true in Salonika was generally true throughout the Judeo-Spanish-speaking communities. For example, the belief in the "evil eye" was a basic reality of life for the Sephardim. Aside from references to the evil eye in classical rabbinic sources, the Jews also shared this notion with the Muslims and Christians among whom they lived. The evil eye was popularly believed to "empty palaces and fill graves." Since this malicious power was activated by envy, it was necessary to underrate or conceal anything that might attract the jealousy of others who might "put the evil eye." It was common practice for people not to praise a beautiful baby or a precious object, since such praise might be construed to be envious, that is, evoking the evil eye. Instead, admiration was expressed through subterfuge, such as denigrating the object or making a neutral, indirect comment. A popular exclamation among Muslims, also commonly used by Jews, was *mashallah*, that is, whatever God wishes. Saying *mashallah* was a way of voicing approval without bringing on fears of the evil eye. Antidotes against the evil eye included garlic, rue, and blue beads.

One who believed that he had been stricken by the evil eye could become quite ill physically and emotionally. A common method of curing this condition was known as *enseredura,* or "isolation." The victim of the evil eye was locked in a room toward the end of a lunar month. The one performing the cure would speak with the patient, just after midnight. The patient would be asked to name the person who had cast the evil eye on him/her. The healer then went to the named person's home, washed the steps of the house, collected the water used in this washing, and brought it back to the patient. The patient, by drinking some of this water, was thereby freed from the power of the evil eye.

A variant cure entailed the patient drinking a concoction made of sweet marjoram, orange blossoms, and sugar at sundown on the first day of isolation. This drink was taken again at midnight and at noon of the next day. On the third day, the patient drank mocha and then went to a hot bath, where a sulfur solution was smeared on his/her body. These ceremonies were accompanied by appropriate incantations designed to ward off evil spirits.

Since most inhabitants of the Ottoman Empire had brown eyes, a popular belief had it that blue eyes could be dangerous. To offset the damage that might be caused by meeting someone with blue eyes, various defenses were utilized. One could wear blue beads, especially those that were fashioned to resemble blue eyes. Some people were so afraid of blue eyes that they would not let their children marry anyone so endowed.

When a person was critically ill, relatives or friends offered a *korban,* or "sacrifice." A cow or lamb was brought to a ritual slaughterer. Blood from the slaughtered animal would be rubbed on the door of the sick person's house. Meat from the animal was distributed to the poor. Another practice to heal the sick was known as *encender el kal,* "lighting the lamps in the synagogue." Relatives would provide the oil for the lamps. They associated this procedure with miraculous cures.

By the mid-nineteenth century, folk superstitions were so deeply entrenched in the community that "modernizers" faced a daunting challenge in their efforts to promote a rationalistic approach to life. The old traditional ways of the Sephardim, while containing so many valuable cultural treasures, also fostered notions that encouraged superstition and retarded adaptation to the modern world.

Confronting Modernity

By the early nineteenth century, the Judeo-Spanish-speaking Jews of the Ottoman Empire had sunk to their lowest economic, political, and cultural levels. Although their inner lives were marked by feelings of self-worth, pride, religious meaning, optimism, and family and communal solidarity, their external conditions were often deplorable. The great challenge was to find ways to ameliorate their negative material situation, without destroying their positive spiritual strengths. Could modernization be achieved while maintaining the virtues of traditional patterns of life?

The Changing Political Context

The reduced situation of the Jews during the early nineteenth century was a reflection of the general decline of the Ottoman Empire. The masses of Muslims and Christians also suffered due to the political, economic, and military failures of the empire. When Mahmud II became sultan in 1808, he initiated a process of reform intended to strengthen the central government and improve the conditions of the people.

In 1826, Mahmud II successfully suppressed the Janissaries and other allied military corps. The Janissaries had been a major factor in Ottoman military might for nearly five centuries. They were a bastion of conservatism, strongly opposed to the modernizing reforms suggested by the sultan. Ottomans and westerners alike agreed that the suppression of the Janissaries was a watershed, opening a new era for the empire.

The period from 1839 to 1876 became known as the *tanzimat* and was marked by significant reforms. The central government was revitalized, and the military was reorganized. Efforts were made to improve roads, communications, health facilities, schools, agriculture, and economic enterprises.[1]

In the 1840s, legal reforms were introduced with the intent of granting equality to non-Muslims. The hope was to create a united Ottoman population loyal to the state, rather than to maintain separate autonomous *millets* (self-governing communities, organized on the basis of religious and ethnic background). In 1856, a decree was issued conferring citizenship rights to non-Muslims, including Jews. This policy of liberalization was not appreciated by the Muslim population at large. A high government official, Cevdet Pasha, described various reactions:

> In accordance with this *ferman* [decree] Muslim and non-Muslim subjects were to be made equal in all rights. This had a very adverse effect on the Muslims.... Many Muslims began to grumble: "Today we have lost our sacred national rights, won by the blood of our fathers and forefathers.... This is a day of weeping and mourning for the people of Islam." As for the non-Muslims, this day ... was a day of rejoicing. But the patriarchs and other spiritual chiefs were displeased.... Some Greeks objected to this, saying: "The government has put us together with the Jews. We were content with the supremacy of Islam." Only on the faces of a few of our Frenchified gentry dressed in the garb of Islam could expressions of joy be seen. Some notorious characters of this type were seen and heard to say: "If the non-

Muslims are spread among the Muslims, neighborhoods will become mixed, the price of our properties will rise, and civilized amenities will expand." On this account they expressed satisfaction.[2]

In 1869, a new citizenship law granted full rights to all subjects of the Sultan, including non-Muslims. This law provided additional legal strength to the earlier decree in 1866. The 1876 constitution strove to diminish divisions within Ottoman society, so that all residents would feel primary loyalty to the central government. A number of Jews entered political life and were elected to the parliament.[3]

Although the Ottoman government extended rights to its residents and sought to modernize its bureaucracy, it was plagued with numerous problems. The empire was literally coming apart. Serbia gained autonomy in 1830 and full independence in 1878. Greece became a sovereign state in 1832. Romania became independent in 1878. Montenegro, Bulgaria, and Albania were also all independent by the early twentieth century. European colonial powers wrested territories from the Ottomans, including Cyprus, Egypt, Bosnia, Herzegovina, Algeria, and Tunisia. Italy took control of the Dodecanese islands and Libya after a war with Turkey in 1911.[4]

The political and military turmoil affected Jews, along with the rest of the Ottoman population. With so many nation-states coming into existence, Jews now found themselves under governments other than Ottoman. Instead of living in a relatively benign Muslim state that was trying to expand their rights, they were now living with minority status in Christian-dominated countries.

The Winds of Change

One of the results of the Ottoman reforms was the establishment of the office of chief rabbi, *haham bashi*, as the religious head of the Jews of Istanbul. Until 1835, the Jews did not have an officially recognized chief rabbi. Rabbi Abraham Levi was appointed to this new position, serving as the civil and religious head of the Jewish community. Yet, many Jews were not ready to accept the leadership of a rabbi appointed by the government. In due time, though, the office gained the general support of the community; highly regarded rabbinic scholars were appointed to the post. By 1864, the office of *haham bashi* was firmly established.[5] Other large Jewish communities also introduced the office of *haham bashi*, although these rabbis tended to be subservient in status to the chief rabbi in Istanbul. In 1909, after the Young Turk Rebellion, Rabbi Haim Nahum was given the title of "Chief Rabbi of All the Jews of the Capital and Its Dependencies and of All the Jews Resident in the Ottoman Empire." He held this post until 1920 and was the only rabbi to have had this title.

As the Jews gained political status with the establishment of the office of chief rabbi, and as they were granted more rights during the period of *tanzimat,* they also experienced internal influences toward westernization. A major impetus came from Jews of Italian origin, known among Turkish Jews as *Francos.* Among the leading families of the *Francos* were Camondo, Allatini, Fernandez, Modiano, and Morpurgo. These Italian Jewish families had come to the Ottoman Empire during the seventeenth and eighteenth centuries for commercial reasons. They were under the protection of foreign consuls and enjoyed preferential taxation in trade. They remained relatively aloof from the local Jews and viewed themselves as part of the mercantile class of Italians rather than as Ottoman Jews.

By the mid-nineteenth century, though, they became increasingly interested in spreading western education and culture among Ottoman Jewry. These Italian Jews reflected the growing impact of the Haskalah (Jewish Enlightenment) movement, which had taken root among European Jews during the late eighteenth and early nineteenth centuries. The Haskalah generally called for a westernization and modernization of Jewish institutions.

A letter by three *Franco* bankers of Salonika, published in the *Archives Israelites* in 1853, noted:

We wish with all our hearts that our emerging relationship might bring some benefit to our poor coreligionists of this city, who, by their numbers and their misery, by their crass ignorance and by their inferior position to people of other religions, have urgent need of help, support and enlightenment from all our coreligionists whom fortune and the benefits of civilization have put in a position of being useful to their brethren.[6]

The most influential of the *Francos* was Count Abraham Camondo. His family had come to Istanbul from Venice in the seventeenth century and had risen to financial prominence. Abraham led his family bank to new heights and became the most important Jewish financial figure in the Ottoman Empire. He was behind the establishment of a new school in Istanbul in 1854 that taught Turkish, Hebrew, Italian, and French. This was the first Jewish school in Turkey that systematically taught languages other than Hebrew and Judeo-Spanish.[7]

While the school quickly attracted students and gained communal support, it also drew the ire of traditionalists, who feared that the school was too "modern" and not religious enough. Rabbi Yitzhak Acrish spearheaded the opposition, calling on parents to withdraw their children from the new school. He went so far as to visit Count Camondo and excommunicate him. Camondo retaliated by having the rabbi thrown into prison. Rabbi Acrish suffered the humiliations of prison life for a short time before masses of Jews marched to the sultan's palace and asked for the rabbi's release. The sultan acceded to their petition.[8] A compromise was eventually worked out between Rabbi Acrish's party and Camondo's school, ensuring that religious instruction would be maintained and that a suitable number of rabbis would be on staff to guarantee faithfulness to religious traditions.

Aside from the efforts of the *Francos* and external European Jewish individuals and organizations, the indigenous Ottoman Jewish population itself showed some signs of internal revitalization.

It became clear to many leaders that the Jewish educational system had to be upgraded. The traditional *meldar* was simply inadequate to provide boys with a practical education that could lead to meaningful employment, and it neglected the education of girls entirely.

The unsatisfactory educational opportunities in the Jewish schools led some parents to enroll their children in schools run by Christian missionaries. The London Society for Promoting Christianity Among the Jews opened its first school in Izmir in 1829. It founded two schools in Istanbul in 1855. The Church of Scotland also opened missionary schools in Izmir in 1846 and Istanbul in 1873. The missionary schools provided good general education as well as instruction in Christian teachings. To induce Jewish parents to enroll their children, the missionaries offered generous scholarship assistance and other material incentives. These schools attracted hundreds of Jewish students, although very few of them ever converted to Christianity. Missionary zeal also led to their publication of Ladino translations of the Hebrew Bible and Christian Bible, a very clever way of influencing unsuspecting Jews. Missionaries distributed these Ladino language texts for free, in the hope of gaining converts. While these publication efforts resulted in very few, if any, conversions of Jews, they put the Jewish community on notice that their own educational efforts needed to be intensified.[9]

The Ottoman government sought to attract Jewish students to state-sponsored schools. The Imperial School of Medicine, established in 1827, graduated its first Jewish student in 1834. To increase Jewish enrollment, the school employed a rabbi in 1847 to supervise daily religious services and to oversee a kitchen that prepared kosher food for Jewish students. In that year, fifteen Jewish students attended the medical school along with about three hundred Muslims, forty Greeks, and twenty-nine Armenians. In 1848, Jewish enrollment grew to twenty-four students and continued to increase in subsequent years. Jewish doctors rose to prominence in the armed forces, in civil administration, and as faculty members in the medical school itself.[10]

Jewish students were encouraged to enroll as trainees in the Translation Bureau, in the Imperial Lycee of Galatasaray, and in other institutions of higher education. Jews increasingly entered the learned professions and government service.[11]

Although the *meldar* system of education was slow to adapt to the changing realities, it did show signs of recognition that Jewish students needed a more sophisticated and diverse curriculum to prepare them for higher education and more productive economic lives. At the same time, it maintained the centrality of religious studies.

Even in religious studies, though, the old-fashioned rote system gave way to some extent to newer pedagogic methods. A significant example of this phenomenon was the publication in 1860 of a Ladino textbook for students (aimed at boys of pre–bar mitzvah age, eleven and twelve). Entitled *Sefer Tov ve-Yafeh* (*Good and Proper Book*), it was authored by an educator in Craiova, David ha-Levy.[12] The book provides religious instruction by means of a dialogue between a teacher and student and has discussions relating to one's duties to God, to fellow human beings, and to oneself.

The first section of the book teaches that God is one and omnipotent, aware of all our thoughts and deeds, and goes on to discuss the relationship between God and people. Since all human beings descend from Adam and Eve, we are all members of one family; we are obligated to care for the well-being of all human beings, whether Jewish or non-Jewish.

The textbook then lists the Ten Commandments; the books of the Torah, the Prophets, and the Writings; and the Thirteen Principles of Faith according to Maimonides. It describes commandments between humans and God (e.g., *tsitsit*, tefillin, recitation of the *Sh'ma*, prayer) and stresses the need for proper devotion during prayer. The book provides brief descriptions of all the holy days, festivals, and fast days and reminds students that these days should be marked by Torah study and synagogue attendance.

The second part of the textbook focuses on commandments governing interpersonal relationships: respect for teachers, parents, sages, and elders; the obligations to give charity and help the needy, console mourners, accompany funeral processions, redeem captives, receive guests, and increase peace among people.

The book's third part relates to our obligations to ourselves. The three main categories are health, occupation, and proper conduct.

The book then includes a number of proverbs/sayings, under the rubric *divrei hahamim* (words of the sages). The following are some examples:

> There is no rose without thorns; there is no good without evil.
> Don't respond to the words you hear from an enemy, so that he does not tell you something even worse.
> He is called happy who has satisfaction from the success of others.
> The greatest success of a person is to correct his errors.
> Religion is a means for achieving true wisdom; and one who uses [religion] for personal advantage is a hypocrite.
> Whoever does not understand a foreign language does not understand his own [language] either.
> The one who pays has credit. One who gives too much credit will be fooled often.
> Cleanliness of the body reflects the cleanliness of the soul.
> There is no greater error than not wanting to correct your error.
> The best doctor is nature, time, and patience.
> Ignorance and slothfulness are the greatest evils.

The book follows with a section on bar mitzvah, including sample bar mitzvah speeches. Then comes a section on the laws of tefillin; laws relating to the New Moon and special Shabbatot; information about the days when holidays can and cannot fall; rules relating to the Torah portions of the week and when two portions are read; and Torah readings for holidays.

Finally, the author includes a section on wisdom and faith. Along with knowledge of the sacred texts, students should be versed in science: how the body functions, the workings of nature. The more we know about the wonders of the natural world, the more we will appreciate the greatness of God. Most important for the attainment of wisdom, though, is a sound knowledge of religion. "The true wisdom is to know God and to serve Him, and one must know Him in order to serve Him." The book closes with a Ladino poem about the prophet Jonah.

This short textbook is remarkable for its pleasant style and for its comprehensiveness. Moreover, it clearly aims at deepening the students' appreciation of religious practices, so that they will observe the commandments with proper devotion. It deals not only with ritual observances, but with philosophic issues, character development, and love of education and wisdom. It sees religion as the key to a virtuous, healthful, and respectful life. In short, this book provides the guidelines for a sophisticated religious world-view, in which the truly religious person is one who serves God and his fellow human beings sincerely, with good manners, as a genuine "gentleman."

This textbook was progressive for its time and indeed could be used profitably in Jewish schools today. Jacques Kabuli, a modern-minded educator who worked for the Alliance Israélite Universelle, published in 1910 (Izmir) and reprinted in 1924 (Rhodes) a textbook that was clearly based on the 1860 textbook prepared by David ha-Levy. Entitled *Livro di Instrucsion Religiosa* (*Book of Religious Instruction*), its publication in the twentieth century by Kabuli was testimony to the book's modern spirit and pedagogical methods.

If the winds of change were apparent in the school system, they were also making some stirrings within traditional rabbinic circles. Figures such as Rabbi Yehudah Bibas (1780–1852) and Rabbi Yehudah Alkalai (1798–1879) challenged the dominant midrashic/kabbalistic approach that fostered passivity. Both were early proponents of the return of the Jews to their Holy Land and the reestablishment of Jewish sovereignty there. Rabbi Bibas, originally from Gibraltar and serving as rabbi in Corfu, called on Jews to study the wisdom of the world—not just Torah—so that they could raise their cultural and economic levels. He even advocated that Jews should develop military skills, so as to strengthen themselves against their enemies. Rabbi Bibas lamented the superstition and ignorance among Jews, and he singled out Polish Jewry as being particularly engulfed by these vices. He argued that solid education and a strong work ethic would enable the Jews to succeed in life and reemerge as an independent nation in the Land of Israel.[13]

Rabbi Alkalai, born in Sarajevo, published his first work in 1834. Entitled *Sh'ma Yisrael*, he called on rabbis to urge members of their communities to emigrate to the Land of Israel and to work for the reestablishment of Jewish nationhood in the ancestral homeland. Rabbi Alkalai devoted his life to generating a spirit of activism among the Jews. He issued many publications, in Hebrew and Ladino, and traveled extensively especially among the Sephardic communities. He was not only idealistic, but was pragmatic as well. He recognized the need for political and economic support for the Jewish return to the Land of Israel. He favored Jews establishing factories in Israel and engaging in agriculture.

> The way of the Torah is to command a person to do all in his power according to natural law. Whatever cannot be achieved by natural exertion will be completed by a miracle. Therefore, the Torah and our own intelligence instruct us to do all that we can do by our natural exertions; the rest will be completed by a miracle.[14]

He criticized pietists who opposed practical steps to material advancement:

> And those pious ones who prevent labor and trades and use of foreign languages, who say with full mouth that Jerusalem was only created for Torah study—if their intention is acceptable, their deeds are not acceptable. It is impossible

to behave in this world as though it were the world-to-come, where there is no need for eating and drinking.[15]

While the activism of Rabbis Bibas and Alkalai did not immediately overturn the traditional quietism of the rabbinic establishment, it did represent the emergence of new ways of thinking. It called on the Sephardim to take practical steps to improve their lot, to broaden their education, and to work for the reestablishment of a national Jewish homeland in Israel. These ideas and attitudes eventually found adherents and laid the foundations for a more activist Sephardic population in the coming generations.

The Alliance Israélite Universelle

The Alliance Israélite Universelle was founded in 1860 by French Jews who sought to improve the political and cultural status of the Jewish people. The Alliance worked for the emancipation of Jewish communities throughout the world and strove to combat anti-Semitism wherever it arose. The centerpiece of its mission was the establishment of modern, progressive schools throughout the Muslim world, where Jewish children could receive a western education steeped in French language and culture.

The Alliance leadership looked upon their coreligionists in the Muslim world, including the Ottoman Empire, as a humiliated and backward group that needed to be saved from their misery and ignorance. Alliance leaders assumed that an infusion of French culture would "modernize" their benighted coreligionists and improve their lives dramatically.

In appealing for support for its mission, the Alliance issued a statement reflecting its essential ideology:

If you believe that a great number of your coreligionists, overcome by twenty centuries of misery, of insults and prohibitions, can find again their dignity as men, win the dignity of citizens; if you believe that one should moralize those who have been corrupted, and not condemn them; enlighten those who have been blinded, and not abandon them; raise those who have been exhausted, and not rest with pitying them; defend those who have been calumnied, and not remain silent; rescue all those who have been persecuted, and not only talk about the persecution ... if you believe in all these things, Jews of the world, come hear our appeal, join our society and give us your help.[16]

The first school established by the Alliance was in Tetuan in 1862. In 1865 it opened a school in Volos, and in 1867 a school in Edirne. Soon thereafter, schools were opened in Salonika, Izmir, and Istanbul (Haskoy, Balat, and Galata). Within several decades, nearly 50 schools were established throughout Ottoman Turkey, and by 1913 the Alliance ran 183 schools attended by 43,700 pupils in an area that stretched from Morocco in the west to Iran in the east. The impact of the Alliance schools on the lives of their students and local communities was dramatic and far ranging.

All of the schools were closely linked to the Central Committee in Paris. The Central Committee issued directives and provided financial support, saw to the training and hiring of directors and teachers for the schools, oversaw the curriculum, and maintained ongoing communications with the school administrations. The reports of the schoolmasters described the conditions of the local Jewish communities, the needs of the schools and their students, the interrelationships between the schools and the local Jewish populations, and the terrible state of education among Jews prior to the advent of the Alliance schools.[17]

Along with French language and culture, the schools taught other European languages as well as Turkish. Instruction was offered in skills that were needed to gain meaningful employment; apprenticeship programs were established. The Alliance opened separate schools for boys and for girls, hence offering girls their first opportunity for formal education.

The success of the Alliance system, however, did not come without strong opposition from religious traditionalists. Many felt that the Alliance schools were more concerned with westernizing their students than with providing proper religious instruction. To be sure, the Alliance schools did teach Hebrew and topics in Jewish religion; yet, the schools seemed to place more value on being "modern" than on being religious. While the level of cooperation and/or antagonism varied from community to community, the Alliance clearly had to deal with the feelings of the local Jews.

As more students were "Frenchified" in the Alliance schools, new cultural divisions surfaced within the Sephardic communities. Some of the more "progressive" Sephardim came to see French as the language of culture; Judeo-Spanish was viewed as an archaic, corrupt language that lacked relevance in the modern world. Moreover, the Alliance community tended to be more secularized than the traditional religious community.

As the Alliance schools attracted more students, the traditionalists found it necessary to upgrade the curriculae of their own schools. The result was that more and more Jewish students—boys and girls—were receiving a better education than had been available before. Rabbis and educators of the traditionalist camp were also among the modernist leaders in educational reform. Such figures included Israel Moshe Hazan, Eliyahu Hazan, Yehudah Nehama, Reuben Eliyahu Israel, Jacques Kabuli, and Nissim Behar.[18] These, and others like them, promoted a genuine religious humanism that blended commitment to religious tradition while advocating a broadening of intellectual perspective by studying works of general wisdom and science.

Other Signs of Modernization

The second half of the nineteenth century witnessed other signs of modernization among Ottoman Jewry. Dr. Esther Benbassa has noted the emergence of new associations among the

Sephardim—groups of Haskalah (Jewish Enlightenment) thinkers, Alliance committees, Zionist clubs.[19] These associations were often "secular," that is, not organic parts of the religious communal structure.

Sephardic writers and intellectuals found new outlets for their literary creativity in the burgeoning field of journalism. The first Ladino newspaper—*La Buena Esperanza*—was published in Izmir in 1842, by Raphael Uziel. Other important Ladino editors included Alexander Benguiat, Elia Carmona, and David Fresco.[20] Ladino newspapers were soon being published throughout the Judeo-Spanish world. They not only provided news, but also opinion, humor, advice, poetry, fiction, historical essays, and more. Drs. Benbassa and Rodrigue list seventy-five Jewish newspapers and periodicals—almost all in Ladino—that circulated within the Ottoman Empire from the mid-nineteenth through the early twentieth centuries.[21]

A secular Ladino literature also emerged, featuring novels, short stories, poetry, and essays. The popularity of this new literature is evident in the publication list of the Jewish publishing houses. In Istanbul, for example, the Jewish publishers issued 138 titles between 1799 and 1900; 106 of them were in Ladino. Whereas in the previous century the vast majority of publications were in Hebrew and on religious themes, the nineteenth-century list is dominated by Ladino titles, many of which are journals/newspapers, novels, and poetry. Of the 138 titles published from 1901 to 1936, almost all were in Ladino. These included 82 works of fiction and drama, 9 journals/newspapers, and other assorted publications of poetry, history, and educational works. Ladino publications included translations of works of world literature, especially from the French, as well as Ladino translations of modern Hebrew literature.

The educational, cultural, economic, and political revival of Ottoman Jewry advanced unevenly. Yet, by the end of the nineteenth century, at least one thoughtful observer was enthusiastic about the situation of the Jews. Gabriel Arie, a Bulgarian Jew who headed the Alliance school in Izmir, wrote in 1893:

What strikes a Bulgarian when he enters Turkey is, before everything else, the air of freedom that one breathes.... The Jews, in particular, can quite justifiably consider themselves in this country as the happiest among all their coreligionists in the world.[22]

In spite of the progress reflected in Arie's remarks, the general condition of Ottoman Jewry was problematic. Poverty was still widespread. Intracommunal strife was growing. The Ottoman Empire continued to deteriorate. The Young Turk Rebellion of 1908 set the stage for the development of Turkey as a modern state, but the process of stabilizing the government and country was arduous. In its drive to secure a constitutional government, the new regime imposed compulsory military service on all its subjects, including Jews. Since the Turkish military made little provision for Jews to maintain their religious observances, traditionalists saw this new law as a threat to Jewish religious life.

Turkey became embroiled in the Turko-Italian War in 1911, followed very soon by the Balkan Wars of 1912–13. Turkey was defeated in these wars and was forced to cede territory to its enemies. The Balkan allies battled among themselves for the distribution of the newly won territories. In July 1913, all-out war involved Rumania, Greece, Serbia, and Bulgaria, ending with a treaty at Bucharest in August. The Jewish populations in Turkey and the Balkans—along with the rest of the population—were subjected to disastrous conditions.

When the dust had settled from the Balkan Wars, the tragic situation of the Jews became quite apparent. Poverty was rampant. Istanbul and Salonika were crowded with refugees from the war zones. Major cities of Sephardic settlement, such as Monastir, Janina, Castoria, Kavala, and Edirne, were severely hit by the wars. The Jews of Bulgaria were compelled to appeal to European and American Jewry for assistance. Many thousands of Jews were in miserable conditions.[23]

To make matters worse, the nation-states that had broken away from the Ottoman Empire had negative attitudes toward their Jewish populations. Jews were suspected as having been loyal to the Ottoman government (which they were) and were therefore subjected to various anti-Jewish manifestations. Anti-Semitic legislation in Serbia in 1846 and 1861 banned Jewish settlement in rural areas and led to the migration of Jews to Belgrade. (In 1888, these laws were rescinded, but by then the demographic changes had already taken place.) During the 1878 Bulgarian war of independence, Jews were victims of large-scale attacks by Bulgarian and Russian soldiers; most of the Jewish quarters in the cities were burned down, and thousands of Jews fled to Istanbul. Anti-Semitic outbreaks also occurred in Salonika at the hands of the Greek army, leading many Jews to flee. A great fire in 1917 razed most of the Jewish quarters of Salonika, and the government then expropriated Jewish-owned land, providing very little compensation to the owners. After Turkey's own war of independence between 1920 and 1922, it entered a period of xenophobia that lasted into the 1940s. All non-Muslims, including Jews, were dismissed from public employment in 1923.[24]

After more than six hundred years, the Ottoman Empire came to an end with the signing of the Treaty of Lausanne in 1923. This treaty followed the Turkish Independence War (1919–22) and determined the boundaries of modern Turkey and Greece.

During the late nineteenth and early twentieth centuries, the Judeo-Spanish communities were in the midst of profound change. They were moving away from the almost fatalistic view of life that had dominated their thinking at least since the generations after Sabbatai Sevi. There were growing signs of activism, modernization, and westernization. Increasing numbers of Sephardim were drawn to Zionism and its promise of Jewish self-determination in their own historic homeland. Many young Sephardim no longer were content to live in the economically and politically troubled Ottoman Empire; they started to consider emigration to lands that offered greater opportunity for advancement.

By the end of the nineteenth century, Turkish Jews began moving to Egypt, where they believed they could find greater

freedom, security, and business opportunities. Early in the twentieth century, thousands of Turkish Jews—mostly young people—
emigrated to the United States, the Land of Israel, and cities in
Africa, Europe, and Latin America. The out-migration of Turkish
Jews continued throughout the twentieth century. In 1904, there
were about 147,000 Jews in Turkey. In 1927, the first census conducted in the Turkish Republic counted only about 82,000 Jews.
The 1935 census counted about 79,000, while the 1945 census listed
about 77,000 Jews. (The Jews of Turkey were protected by the government and were not deported to Nazi concentration camps.) By
1955 the number of Jews had dropped to about 46,000, and by 1965
to about 38,000. In 1972, the number of Jews in Turkey was estimated at about 36,000.[25] By the beginning of the twenty first century, the Jewish population of Turkey had dropped to 20,000 or less.

Within Turkey itself, there was a significant demographic shift
of the Jewish population. Small Jewish communities in towns
throughout the country shrank and disappeared as Jews moved to
the larger Turkish cities. By the latter twentieth century, almost all
the Jews of Turkey were concentrated in Istanbul, with a small community in Izmir and scattered tiny groups of Jews in a few other cities.

The End of Judeo-Spanish Civilization

When Turkish Jews settled in the Land of Israel, the United States,
and elsewhere, they tended to live in close proximity to each other
and to maintain the cultural patterns of their home country. Their
main language of communication continued to be Judeo-Spanish.
They established synagogues, publications, eating establishments,
and societies along the lines of those institutions in "the old country." They tended to marry within their own group.

Yet, the children of these Turkish Sephardic immigrants were
being raised outside of the traditional Jewish communities in Turkey
and the Balkans and had to adapt to their new lands. They attended
schools where Judeo-Spanish was not the language of instruction.
Their classmates were, for the most part, not fellow Turkish

Sephardim. Within a generation, these children of Turkish Sephardic immigrants were becoming full-fledged English-speaking Americans, Hebrew-speaking Israelis, Spanish-speaking Mexicans, and so on. The grandchildren of the Turkish immigrants, with few exceptions, no longer spoke Judeo-Spanish or lived within a predominantly Sephardic milieu.[26] Even in Turkey, with the establishment of the Turkish Republic in the early 1920s, Jewish youngsters increasingly attended Turkish schools, spoke Turkish rather than Judeo-Spanish, and drifted further away from the old Sephardic traditions that had characterized their grandparents' generation.

By the mid-twentieth century, Judeo-Spanish civilization was coming to an end as a living organism. Some elders still conversed in Judeo-Spanish, but almost none of the younger generations spoke the language fluently. Even those who did no longer used the language as their main means of communication, since there were so few other native speakers. This pattern continued into the twenty-first century, when many of the elder native speakers of the language had died.

The Holocaust was a decisive factor in the destruction of Judeo-Spanish life. The vicious Nazis and their collaborators massacred millions of European Jews, with savagery unparalleled in human history. Among the victims of the Holocaust were many thousands of Sephardim. Over 90 percent of Greek Jewry perished in the Nazi concentration camps. The historic and vibrant Jewish community of Salonika was reduced to ashes, as were so many other Sephardic communities, including those in Monastir, Sarajevo, and Rhodes. While the Jews of Turkey and Bulgaria were spared from the Nazi deportations, most of the Jews in the Balkan countries were forced into concentration camps and were murdered.

Functionally, we have witnessed the death of Judeo-Spanish civilization. Judeo-Spanish is fading away as a living tongue. Although there has been a resurgence of interest in singing Ladino songs and teaching classes in the Ladino language, it cannot be denied that Judeo-Spanish has crossed the line from being a living language to a dead language that still evokes nostalgic interest.[27] Yet, while the Judeo-Spanish language and civilization have effectively come to an end, they have left a precious and lasting legacy that can have meaning to future generations.

The era of westernization that set in during the latter nineteenth century offered the promise of a revitalized, modern Sephardic Jewry in the Ottoman Empire. In shaking off the cultural cobwebs of the past, proponents of westernization hoped to stimulate the emergence of an educated and enlightened Turkish Jewry, freed of its old folkways and superstitions.

Without realizing it at the time, though, the "progressives" were in fact laying the foundation for the unraveling of Judeo-Spanish civilization. They promoted French as the language of culture and viewed Judeo-Spanish as a relic of a failed civilization. They seemed to care more about economic, cultural, and political advancement, rather than about helping young people maintain their loyalty to their religious traditions and historic folk patterns.

The traditionalists were not successful enough in preparing young people for productive, practical lives in the modern world. Their teachings grew increasingly out of touch with the new generations.

Moreover, the world around them was changing. The Ottoman Empire was collapsing. Wars and civil unrest were unsettling. The opportunities for emigration expanded, and young Sephardim were now willing to take their futures into their own hands by moving to new lands.

Judeo-Spanish civilization was able to flourish for centuries because of the distinctive sociological pattern of life in the Ottoman Empire. Jews formed an autonomous community of their own, with their own schools, synagogues, publications, court system, etc. They lived in their own neighborhoods and spoke their own language. They were *in* the empire, but not *of* the empire.

The reforms of the *tanzimat* were actually a double-edged sword as far as the Jews were concerned. For "progressives," the reforms were a step in the direction of increased rights for Jews, so that Jews could be citizens equal to all others in the empire. Yet, this political gain was counterbalanced by the loss of the very communal insularity that had guaranteed Jewish autonomy over the past centuries. For "progressives," the breakdown in traditional religious authority was a step toward personal freedom. Yet, it had been the religious authority—its institutions, rules, and customs—that had formed the fabric of Jewish life for centuries. When the religious patterns were broken, so were many of the deep emotional ties Sephardim had to their civilization. In seeking to become modern, they were being asked to sacrifice the "old-fashioned" way of life that had provided meaning and structure to their communities. While a few of the traditionalists attempted to bridge the gap between traditionalism and modernity, the sociological and political forces for change were too powerful.

Judeo-Spanish civilization has run its course in history as a living, dynamic organism. During its nearly five hundred years, it was a vital expression of the lives of hundreds of thousands of Jews. As it reaches the end of its course in history, what lasting lessons does it provide for the future generations?

10

Lasting Lessons

We have reviewed the nearly five centuries of Judeo-Spanish civilization and have explored aspects of the inner life of the Sephardim—their beliefs, customs, and attitudes. The intellectual elite of the Sephardim have left an impressive legacy of works in Halakhah, Kabbalah, midrash, poetry, and ethical literature. The common folk produced and maintained a rich folkloric culture that was, in many ways, interrelated with the teachings of the sages. The "intellectual" wisdom and the folk wisdom shared common values and assumptions; together they shaped the overall nature of Judeo-Spanish civilization.

Interiority

Sephardic culture strengthened the individual's inner life, fostering self-respect, self-confidence, self-reliance, and a sense of personal pride. Even when external conditions of life were problematic, Sephardim drew courage from the belief that they were descendants of the aristocracy of Judea. As Jews, they were God's chosen people, with a special mission in this world. As Sephardim, they were the elite of the Jewish people. If their material situation was unsatisfactory, they had perfect confidence that one day they would be restored to their former glory. They did not see themselves as a lowly, humiliated group, but rather as an aristocracy that temporarily had fallen on hard times.

Sephardic inner life included a profound reverence for holiness. Scholars and laymen alike read the *Zohar* on a regular basis, seeing in this classic work of Kabbalah a connection with divine mysteries. Rabbi Hayyim Yosef David Azulai underscored the importance of the *Zohar*, even for those who did not understand what they were reading:

> The study of the *Zohar* is above any other study, even if one does not understand what it says, and even if he errs in his reading. It is a great corrective for the soul. Even though the Torah is composed of the names of God, nevertheless it is clothed in a number of stories. One who reads and understands the stories, pays attention to the obvious meaning. But the book of the *Zohar* is composed of the ultimate mysteries themselves, revealed. One who reads them knows that they are the mysteries and secrets of the Torah though they are not understood due to the shortcomings of the perceiver and the profundity of that which is being perceived.[1]

The very awareness of the holiness of the *Zohar* was in itself a key to a deeper spiritual life.

Awareness of holiness showed itself in various ways. It endowed life with a sense of mystery; it taught one to feel God's presence at all times; it promoted spiritual humility. It manifested itself in customs: kissing the hands of rabbis, living symbols of the Torah, and receiving a blessing from them; visiting the graves of saintly people, as a sign of respect; striving to spend time in the Holy Land of Israel, visiting and even settling there.

The quality of holiness was attained through the practice of *hitbod'dut*, "meditation," making private inner space for oneself. Rabbi Eliezer Papo described *hitbod'dut* as the foundation stone of holiness, helping one to think pure thoughts and awakening one's love and fear of God.

> It is good for a person to set aside a place that will be just for himself and no others, so that he can meditate there to study and acquire the way of holiness. If he only has one house with his family, let him arise at night while they are sleeping, and then let him be alone with his Creator. For in one hour of private meditation [*hitbod'dut*] he can learn and understand and acquire the way of holiness more than in an entire day.[2]

The goal was to be able to feel alone with one's internal thoughts, even when in the presence of others, even when in a crowd.

Rabbi Eliezer Azikri noted in his *Sefer Hareidim* that a person needed to maintain inner calm at all times, not falling into anger or other negative emotions. The Bible (Genesis 5:8) states that "Noah found favor in the eyes of the Lord." Rabbi Azikri cited the Midrash *Ne'alam*, a kabbalistic work, which interpreted the verse based on the meaning of the word *noah*—calm:

> By having one's heart always calm and settled, one finds favor in the eyes of God…. In the following verse, Noah's name is mentioned three times [to indicate] that when one's heart was very settled, he will be calm in his speech, calm in his manner of walking, calm in his deeds.[3]

Optimism, Joy in Life

Sephardim generally maintained an optimistic outlook on life and celebrated the joys of this world even as they longed to be worthy of a place in the world-to-come. Sabbaths and holy days, of course, were times of special rejoicing, with distinctive foods and songs. The Sephardic table was characterized by the many colors of the various vegetables used in Sephardic cuisine—and the special fragrances of the spices and herbs, and freshly baked breads and pastries. Even on weekdays, Sephardim found occasion for celebratory gatherings, with singing and dancing, and enjoying tasty repasts.

The synagogue services were marked by enthusiastic singing of the congregants. Liturgical music was lively and uplifting, rarely somber or melancholy. The communal aspect of synagogue prayer reinforced a feeling of communal solidarity and personal well-being.

Although Sephardic sages produced classic works of ethics and moral guidance, these works did not engender a religious life based on guilt. Yes, atonement was a vital ingredient in life; but God was a loving Parent who welcomed our repentance. God was forgiving, compassionate, kind. Perhaps the relatively sunny outlook of Sephardim was influenced by the fact that most of them lived in sunny Mediterranean climates.

Gracefulness, Good Manners

When Rabbi Moshe Almosnino of sixteenth-century Salonika published *Regimiento de la Vida* (*Regimen for Life*), he was reflecting a deeply held view among Sephardim of the importance of gracefulness and good manners. His concern for proper etiquette was seen as an expression of the religious imperative of respecting others. Sephardic authors, including those who wrote textbooks for children, stressed good manners and proper comportment. Self-respect needed to be accompanied by respect for others.

Homes were decorated with a keen sense of aesthetics. Even the poorest Sephardim took pride in neatness and cleanliness, in beautifully embroidered fabrics; in furnishings and utensils as nice as one could afford. Synagogues were built to as high an aesthetic standard as the community could manage and were maintained with devotion to orderliness and propriety. The concern for aesthetics reflected not merely self-respect and respect for others, but also respect for the Almighty. Professor Daniel Elazar has noted:

In the matter of form, Sephardic emphasis on aesthetics, on external appearance, on symmetry, stands out. Sephardim have a word for it, *kavod*, which every Sephardi learns in Hebrew and in his own regional Jewish language. In Ladino, for example, it is *honor*, a word which carries with it a whole complex of attitudes, values and expectations.[4]

Proportion

Abraham Joshua Heschel noted that Sephardim sought proportion and balance in whatever they undertook. They prided themselves on being less fanatical than other groups of Jews, more tolerant and balanced in their view of life.[5] In describing the culture of the Jews of North Africa, Andre Chouraqui observed that "the Judaism of [even] the most conservative of the Maghreb's Jews was marked by a flexibility, a hospitality, a tolerance." The Jews of North Africa had a "touching generosity of spirit and a profound respect for meditation."[6] These observations applied equally to the Judeo-Spanish communities of Turkey and the Balkan countries. Indeed, Michael Molho, in his study of the customs of the Sephardim of Salonika, noted that Salonika's Jews generally eschewed signs of religious extremism; they were optimistic, tolerant, hospitable, and gracious.[7]

Daniel Elazar has written:

> Sephardim are bewildered by the Ashkenazi pursuit of *humrot* [halakhic stringencies], because they have traditionally sought to balance the requirements of observance with the requirements of living, to achieve a form of religious expression that is balanced and proportionate, that takes into consideration the whole man—not to torture and subordinate him as a basis for religious satisfaction, but to encourage and cultivate the range of human attributes.[8]

Religion and Life

The Sephardic religious worldview kept in mind that Sephardim were not just Jews: they were human beings, with the emotions, interests, and concerns of humanity. Ladino folklore, especially the *romances*, expressed the deepest feelings of love, jealousy, grief, and joy—indeed the entire array of human emotions. Sephardic civilization encompassed all aspects of life in a natural, easygoing manner.

This quality is manifested in a Ladino translation and commentary on *Pirkei Avot* (*Ethics of the Fathers*) prepared by Rabbi Reuben Eliyahu Israel, who served as chief rabbi of the Jewish community of the Island of Rhodes from 1922 until his death in 1932. Born in Rhodes in 1856, Rabbi Israel was a descendant of an outstanding Sephardic rabbinic family that produced rabbis and scholars going back many generations. Rabbi Moshe Israel (c. 1670–1740) was the founder of this family in Rhodes and had been considered one of the great rabbinic scholars of his day.

Rabbi Reuben Eliyahu Israel produced his volume of *Pirkei Avot* with the express idea of popularizing this classic rabbinic work of ethics among those Sephardim who did not understand the Hebrew original. His lucid Ladino translation and commentaries did indeed find a receptive audience.

At the conclusion of his translation and commentaries, Rabbi Israel included a variety of maxims and poems relating to the ethical teachings of Judaism. He also offered his male readers advice on how to deal with women! This included the following, for example:

> He who takes a wife in order to obtain her large dowry writes a divorce to his repose.
> When poverty enters the door, love flies out the window.
> Examine carefully the companion you choose, because the error is one minute but the remorse is a lifetime.
> Praise a woman's beauty in her presence, and she will forgive all your sins.

The significance of this section is not so much the particular advice offered by Rabbi Israel, but the very fact that he chose to include it in this popular book of rabbinic ethics. The treatment of such a "secular" subject in a rabbinic work reveals the Sephardic worldview that dealt with all aspects of life, not simply the "religious."[9]

Dr. Raphael Patai, noted anthropologist and author, described his efforts to establish an organization, in Jerusalem in 1944, dedicated to the study of Jewish folklore and ethnology. The organization planned to publish a quarterly journal, *Edoth.* He visited the two chief rabbis of Israel in the hope of interesting them in this project. He first went to see the Ashkenazic chief rabbi, Isaac Herzog. Patai described plans to collect, record, study, and analyze the folklore and customs of the numerous Jewish ethnic groups living in the Holy Land. He received a lukewarm response from the learned rabbi, who seemed to think that the study of folklore was of very minor significance, especially when compared to the far more important study of Jewish law and sacred texts. Patai was disheartened by his meeting with Rabbi Herzog.

Several days later, he visited Rabbi Benzion Uziel, the Sephardic chief rabbi of Israel. In looking at the books in Rabbi Uziel's office and comparing them to the books in Rabbi Herzog's office, Patai observed:

> The heavy halakhic tomes predominated here too, but there were also many other books, in Hebrew as well as in several European languages, which testified to the Rishon Lezion's [Chief Rabbi's] wide-ranging interests.

Patai explained his project to Rabbi Uziel and was delighted that Rabbi Uziel was entirely familiar with the field of folklore and ethnology.

> In fact, he reminded me of one important area of Sephardi folklore that was still sorely neglected at the time: that of

the *romancero*, the rich corpus of ballads in Ladino…. My suggestion that he become a patron of our society was immediately and unhesitatingly accepted, and when I left his presence, I had the feeling that I had experienced an enriching influence.[10]

Patai found that the Ashkenazic chief rabbi was entirely focused on Halakhah. The Sephardic chief rabbi, though equally gifted and learned in Halakhah, had a broader range of intellectual interests. He valued the study of Jewish folklore and customs, and prized the Ladino tradition of love songs and ballads.

The Sephardic religious worldview encompassed all of life, in an easygoing, natural way. This was true not only among intellectuals like Rabbi Reuben Eliyahu Israel and Rabbi Benzion Uziel, but was also evident among the Sephardic masses. An example may be drawn from the experiences of the German Jewish philosopher Franz Rosenzweig, who visited the Sephardic community in Uskub (Yugoslavia) in 1917. He spent time with the president of the community, whom he described as "a merchant whose manner is very dignified but even more markedly astute." Rosenzweig noted that the family was prosperous and well-educated, but not particularly versed in Jewish texts. While they knew French, they spoke Judeo-Spanish among themselves. What especially impressed Rosenzweig was that "the Jewish way of life is entirely natural to them." They were thoroughly and unapologetically Jewish, clearly proud of their heritage, part of a pervasive folk-civilization.[11] They personified the natural blend of Jewish identity and worldliness inherent in Judeo-Spanish civilization.

Religious Humanism

In his study of Rabbi Israel Moshe Hazan (1807–63), Professor Jose Faur emphasized the religious humanism evident among Sephardic thinkers. These sages were deeply steeped in Jewish learning, but were also open to the insights available from the non-Jewish world.

Jews had their own distinctive religious civilization, but they also shared much in common with the rest of humanity.

Dr. Faur has noted that the Sephardic attitude toward general culture presupposed a dynamic concept of Judaism.

> Judaism is not a static ideal to be maintained by erecting walls that would prevent any meaningful interaction with the general cultural environment. There is a perennial need of interpretation and adaptation of the eternal values of Israel in order to meet the specific conditions of every historical situation.... It is the task of the Jewish sage, in particular, to interpret the key cultural symbols of his own times in light of this mental language, on the one hand, and the constitutive values of Israel, on the other hand.[12]

The Sephardic religious humanism manifested itself in various ways. For one thing, there was a general tolerance for people whose level of religious observance may have been less than perfect. In Sephardic congregations, certainly from the nineteenth century on, pious Jews prayed together with less pious Jews easily and comfortably. While Sephardic communities were characterized by a profound reverence for tradition, they were remarkably nonjudgmental of those members whose personal religious behavior veered from traditional norms. For the most part, Sephardic rabbis tried to win adherents through kindness and compassion rather than by chastisements and threats. The classic Sephardic approach to Halakhah was characterized by the quality of *hesed*, compassion and understanding of the human predicament.

Sephardic tradition generally eschewed extreme positions, trying to keep as many Jews as possible within the fold. It is no accident that Sephardim never broke into various religious movements, as did the Ashkenazim (i.e., Orthodox, Conservative, Reform, Reconstructionist). Sephardim preferred to maintain traditional communities, faithful to Halakhah, while at the same time recognizing a spectrum of religious observance in people's personal lives.

Concluding Comments

Judeo-Spanish civilization has reached its conclusion as a living, dynamic organism. There are no more communities in the world where Judeo-Spanish is the mother tongue of the younger generations, and there is no sociological reason for Judeo-Spanish-speaking communities to emerge in the future.

The death of the language is a result of the new realities of modern times. Sephardim no longer live in isolated enclaves in Turkey or the Balkan countries—or anywhere else. They speak the language of the lands in which they live and mingle with Jews and non-Jews of many backgrounds. Jews of Judeo-Spanish background increasingly marry partners who are not of this background. The old language fades away; the old customs also may be watered down or dropped.

Yet, the vitality of the Judeo-Spanish civilization's historical experience has powerful, ongoing lessons for moderns. We all have much to learn from the courage, pride, and calm wisdom of the historic bearers of the Judeo-Spanish tradition. The inner life of the Sephardim of the Ottoman Empire provides insights for us as we face the challenges of our own lives.

I began this book with reflections about my grandparents, who came to the United States from Turkey and Rhodes during the early twentieth century. My grandfather Romey used to say, based on a kabbalistic teaching, that each person was put on earth to accomplish a unique mission. This is true of individuals—but is also true of civilizations. The Judeo-Spanish community has made vast contributions to Jewish life and lore, yet it now enters a new phase in the fulfillment of its distinctive mission. In this phase, its central teachings and experiences will be translated and incorporated into the general wisdom and culture of the entire Jewish people. The light in the Sephardic dwellings will provide continued illumination and inspiration to all Jews—and indeed to all sensitive and thoughtful students of the human adventure.

Notes

Chapter One: The Inner Life of the Sephardim

1. Louis Hacker, "The Communal Life of the Sephardic Jews in New York City," *Jewish Social Service Quarterly* 3 (December 1926): 33.

2. Dr. Adler's address is in the archives of Congregation Shearith Israel, New York City, in the minute book of the Sisterhood's Oriental Committee.

3. See David de Sola Pool's article, "The Immigration of Levantine Jews into the United States," *Jewish Charities* (June 1914): 12–27. See also chapter 4 of my book, *La America: The Sephardic Experience in the United States* (Philadelphia: Jewish Publication Society, 1982).

4. Comments by David Porter, *Constantinople and Its Environs* (New York, 1835), as quoted by M. J. Benardete; *Hispanic Culture and Character of the Sephardic Jews* (New York: Sepher-Hermon Press and Sephardic House, 1982), 138.

5. C. Oscanyan, *The Sultan and His People* (New York, 1857), 376–79. See Avigdor Levy's introduction to the book he edited, *The Jews of the Ottoman Empire,* (Princeton, NJ: Darwin Press, 1994), 96–97.

6. Louis Bertrand, *Le Mirage Oriental* (Paris, 1910), in J. C. Berchet, *Le Voyage en Orient*, 575.

7. Bertrand Bareilles, *Constantinople—Ses Cites Franques et Levantines* (Paris: Editions Bossard, 1918), 307.

8. A. H. Navon, *Joseph Perez* (Paris: Calman-Levy, 1925), 4.

9. See Marie-Christine Borres-Varol, "The Balat Quarter and Its Image," in *The Jews of the Ottoman Empire*, ed. Avigdor Levy, 633–44.

10. Ibid., 636.

11. Ibid., 641.

12. Ibid., 642–43.

13. This report is found in the Archives of the Alliance Israélite Universelle in Paris, in the files on Rhodes.

14. Semach's letters are in the Archives of the Alliance Israélite Universelle in Paris, in the files on Rhodes. See letters dated November 27, 1901; February 11 and 12, 1902; September 24, 1902; August 13, 1903. See also my book, *The Jews of Rhodes: The History of a Sephardic Community* (New York: Sepher-Hermon Press, 1978), 53.

15. A second, corrected edition, edited by me, was issued by Sepher-Hermon Press and Sephardic House, New York, 1982.

16. Avigdor Levy's introduction to the book he edited, *The Jews of the Ottoman Empire*, 122.

Chapter Two: Iberian Roots

1. Quoted by Bernard Lewis, *The Jews of Islam* (Princeton, NJ: Princeton University Press, 1984), 135–36.

2. Yitzhak Abravanel, *Mayenei ha-Yeshua* (Stettin, 1860), introduction.

3. Yitzhak Abravanel, *Commentary on the Nevi'im Rishonim* (Jerusalem, 1955), in his introduction to Kings.

4. See my book, *Voices in Exile* (Hoboken, NJ: Ktav Publishing House, 1991), 4–6. See also Hayyim Hillel Ben-Sasson, "*Galut u-Geulah be-Einav shel Dor Golei Sefarad,*" in *Sefer ha-Yovel le-Yitshak Baer,* ed. by Sh. Ettinger et al. (Jerusalem, 5721/1961), 23–64; and Simon Bernfeld, *Sefer ha-Demaot* (Berlin, 1924), 2:242ff. See also H. H. Ben-Sasson's article, "*Kinah al Gerush Sefarad,*" *Tarbitz* 3 (1961): 59–71.

5. See Avigdor Levy's introduction to the volume he edited, *Jews of the Ottoman Empire*, 11–12.

6. Solomon Rosanes, *Dibrei Yemei Yisrael be-Togarmah* (Tel Aviv, 1930), 1:203–18, for more on the Romaniots. Eliyahu Mizrahi, *Mayim Amukim* (Salonika, 5570/1809), nos. 1, 2, 24, and 57 deal with tensions caused by differing religious practices among the groups of Jews.

7. Capsali's comments are found in Elias Artom and Humbertus Cassuto, eds., *Sefer Takanoth Candia* (Jerusalem, 1943), 43.

8. D. Frenkel, ed., *Zera Anashim* (Husiyatin, 1902), E. H. no. 4. See Minna Rozen, "Individual and Community in the Jewish Society of the Ottoman Empire: Salonica in the Sixteenth Century," in *Jews of the Ottoman Empire*, ed. Avigdor Levy, 218.

9. Responsa of Rabbi Shemuel de Medina, O. H. no 35.

10. Rosanes, *Dibrei Yemei*, 132–33.

11. Joseph Nehama, *Histoire des Israelites de Salonique* (Paris, 1935), 2:26–27; the English translation is from M. J. Benardete, *Hispanic Culture*, 62–63.

12. Rabbi Yosef b. Moshe mi-Trani, *Tsafenat Pa'aneah* (Venice, 5408/1647), introduction. See Joseph Hacker's article, "The Intellectual Activity of the Jews of the Ottoman Empire during the Sixteenth and Seventeenth Centuries," in *Jewish Thought in the Seventeenth Century*, ed. I. Twersky and B. Septimus (Cambridge, MA: Harvard University Press, 1987), 95–135.

13. Hacker, ibid., 107.

14. David Solomon Sassoon, *Ohel David* (London, 1932), 1:63–66. Quoted by Hacker, ibid., 107–8.

15. Hacker, ibid., 133–35.

16. Ibid., 134.

17. Mark Epstein, "The Leadership of the Ottoman Jews in the Fifteenth and Sixteenth Centuries," in *Christians and Jews in the Ottoman Empire*, ed. Benjamin Braude and Bernard Lewis (New York and London: Holmes and Meier, 1982), 1:110–11.

18. Avigdor Levy's introduction to *Jews of the Ottoman Empire*, 38.

19. Ibid., 35.

20. See Mark Epstein's article, "Leadership of the Ottoman Jews," 105; and his book *The Ottoman Jewish Communities* (Verlag: Freiburg, Klaus, Schwarz, 1980), 100ff.

21. Vicente Roca, *Historia en la qual se trata de la origin y guerras que han tenido los Turcos* (Valencia, 1556), folio li verso; quoted by Lewis, *The Jews of Islam*, 135.

22. Cited by Avigdor Levy in his introduction to *The Jews of the Ottoman Empire*, 27.

23. Ibid., 34–35.

24. Joseph Nehama, *Histoire des Israelites*, 2:39–41; Benardete, *Hispanic Culture*, 65–66.

25. Benardete, ibid., 64–65; see also Max A. Luria, *A Study of the Monastir Dialect of Judeo-Spanish* (New York and Paris: Revue Hispanique, 1930). For a discussion of the Spanish language, known as Hakitia, maintained in Morocco, see Jose Benoliel, *Dialecto Judeo-Hispano-Marroqui O Hakitia* (Madrid: Varona, 1977). For the dominance of Spanish in Rhodes, see my book, *The Jews of Rhodes*, 23.

26. Benardete, ibid., 14.

27. See Herman P. Salomon's article, "Myth or Anti-Myth? The Oldest Accounts Concerning the Origin of Portuguese Judaism at Amsterdam," in his volume, *Two Portuguese Studies* (Braga, 1991).

28. Leon Sciaky, *Farewell to Salonica* (New York: Current Books, 1946), 114–15.

Chapter Three: The Ottoman Milieu

1. Samuel Usque, *Consolation on the Tribulations of Israel*, trans. Martin Cohen (Philadelphia: Jewish Publication Society, 1977), 211, 231.

2. Quoted by Joseph Hacker, "Jewish Autonomy in the Ottoman Empire," in *The Jews of the Ottoman Empire*, ed. Avigdor Levy, 157–58.

3. Ibid., 158.

4. Braude, "Foundation Myths," in *Christians and Jews in the Ottoman Empire*, ed. Braude and Lewis, 75.

5. Charles Berlin, "Elijah Capsali's *Seder Eliyahu Zuta*" (Ph.D. thesis, Harvard University, September 1962), 2:529. See also Elijah Capsali, *Likutim Shonim mi-Sefer Debei Eliyahu*, ed. M. Lattes (Padua, 1869), 47; and my book, *A History of the Jews of Rhodes*, 19.

6. Joseph Hacker, "Ottoman Policy toward the Jews," in *Christians and Jews in the Ottoman Empire*, ed. Braude and Lewis, 1:121.

7. Ibid., 123–24.

8. S. D. Goitein, *Jews and Arabs* (New York: Schocken Books, 1974), 67. For a discussion of the legal status of *dhimmis* in Muslim law, see H. A. R. Gibb and H. Bowen, *Islamic Society and the West* (London: Oxford University Press, 1950), vol. 1, part 1:20f, and part 2:207–61. See also, Reuben Levy, *The Social Structure of Islam* (Cambridge: Cambridge University Press, 1971), 66; and Walter Weiker, *Ottomans, Turks and the Jewish Polity: A History of the Jews of Turkey* (Jerusalem: The Jerusalem Center for Public Affairs, 1992), chap. 3.

9. M. de Thevenot, as quoted by Alfred Rubens, *A History of Jewish Costume* (New York, 1973), 33.

10. Lewis, *The Jews of Islam*, 32.

11. Ibid., 37.

12. Amnon Cohen, *Jewish Life Under Islam: Jerusalem in the Sixteenth Century* (Cambridge, MA: Harvard University Press, 1984), 139.

13. Lewis, *The Jews of Islam*, 59.

14. Cited by Jacob Landau, *Jews in Nineteenth Century Egypt* (New York: New York University Press, 1969), 18–19.

15. See, for example, Braude's article, "Foundation Myths," 70–71.

16. Avigdor Levy's introduction to *Jews in the Ottoman Empire*, 40.

17. G. Sandys, "A Relation of a Journey Begunne, AD 1610," *Purchas' His Pilgrimes* 2:1306.

Chapter Four: Religious Foundations

1. Avraham Yaari, *Ha-Defus ha-Ivri be-Kushta* (Jerusalem: Magnes Press, 1967). Yaari lists all the books published by the Hebrew press in Istanbul, and I have sorted them out according to their categories.

2. H. J. Zimmels, "The Contributions of the Sephardim to the Responsa Literature Till the Beginning of the Sixteenth Century," in *The Sephardi Heritage*, ed. Richard Barnett (New York: Ktav Publishing House, 1971), 394.

3. Yosef Hacker, *"Lidmutam ha-ruhanit shel Yehudei Sefarad be-Sof ha-Meah he-Hamesh Esrei," Sefunot* 17 (5743/1983): 47–48.

4. R. J. Z. Werblowsky, *Joseph Caro* (Philadelphia: Jewish Publication Society, 1977), 286.

5. Joseph Dan, *Jewish Mysticism and Jewish Ethics* (Seattle: University of Washington Press, 1986), 96–97.

6. See my book, *Voices in Exile*, 37–38.

7. Moshe Cordovero, *The Palm Tree of Deborah*, trans. Louis Jacobs (London, 1960), 69.

8. Dan, *Jewish Mysticism*, 100–101.

9. Cordovero, *The Palm Tree of Deborah*, 52–53.

10. See Solomon Schechter, "Safed in the Sixteenth Century," *Studies in Judaism*, 2nd series (Philadelphia: Jewish Publication Society, 1908), 292ff.

11. Maimonides' introduction to *Perek Helek*.

12. *Maamar al Odot Derashot Hazal.*

13. Abraham ibn Migash, *Kevod Elohim* (Jerusalem: Jewish National and University Press, 1976), 51b. See also 57b for an expression of the value of general wisdom.

14. Ibid., 93a–b.

15. Hacker, "The Intellectual Activity of the Jews of the Ottoman Empire during the Sixteenth and Seventeenth Centuries," 118–19.

16. Yehudah Zarco, *Lehem Yehudah*, edited by A. M. Haberman (Jerusalem: Haberman Institute, 1970).

17. Yosef Yaavets, *Or ha-Hayyim*, in *Kol Sifrei Rav Yosef Yaavets* (Jerusalem, 5694/1934), 2:79, 115.

18. Meir ben Gabbai, *Sefer Avodat ha-Kodesh* (Lvov, 1848), 32a–34b.

Chapter Five: Turning Points

1. See Avigdor Levy's introduction to *Jews of the Ottoman Empire*, 71.

2. Ibid., 75.

3. Ibid., 76.

4. Ibid., 76–77.

5. Ibid., 80.

6. Ibid., 71.

7. Bernard Lewis, *The Emergence of Modern Turkey* (London: Oxford University Press, 1961), 23.

8. Abravanel's messianic works were *Ma'yenei ha-Yeshuah; Mashmia Yeshua; Yeshuot Meshiho.* For a discussion of his messianic writings, see Benzion Netanyahu, *Abravanel* (Philadelphia: Jewish Publication Society, 1968), chap. 4.

9. Cited by Gershom Scholem, *Shabbatai Zevi* (Tel Aviv, 1957), 1:15.

10. Hayyim Hillel Ben-Sasson, "*Galut u-geulah be-Einav shel Dor Golei Sefarad,*" in *Sefer Yovel le-Yitzhak Baer* (Jerusalem, 5721/1961), 216–27.

11. See Matt Goldish, *The Sabbatean Prophets* (Cambridge, MA: Harvard University Press, 2004), where he discusses messianic speculations among Christians and Muslims around the time of Sabbatai Sevi.

12. Yaacov Sasportas, *Zizat Novel Zevi*, in back section of his *Ohel Yaacov* (Bnei Brak, 5746/1986), 85a.

13. For more on the life and influence of Sabbatai Sevi, see Gershom Scholem, *Sabbatai Sevi* (Princeton, NJ: Princeton University Press, 1973). For more about the continuing battles relating to Sabbateanism, see Elisheva Carlebach, *The Pursuit of Heresy* (New York: Columbia University Press, 1990).

14. Y. Baer, *Galut* (New York, 1947), 114.

15. M. Hagiz, *Sefat Emet* (Amsterdam, 5647/1887), 17a.

16. Jacob Barnai, "From Sabbateanism to Modernization," in *Sephardi and Middle Eastern Jewries*, ed. H. Goldberg (Bloomington: Indiana University Press, 1996), 75.

17. Solomon Rosanes, *Korot ha-Yehudim be-Turkiah ve-Artsot ha-Kedem* (Sofia, 1937–38), 5:1–2.

18. Solomon Reinach, "Les Juifs d'Orient d'Apres les Geographes et le Voyageurs," *Revue des Etudes Juives* 20 (1890): 98.

19. *The Letters and Works of Lady Mary Wortley Montagu* (London, 1893), 1:283.

20. Avigdor Levy's introduction, *The Jews of the Ottoman Empire*, 90–91.

21. Ezra Malki, *Ein Mishpat* (Istanbul, 5530/1770), H. M. 10.

22. M. Y. Israel, *Yad Yemin* (Izmir, 5619/1858), O. H. 2.

23. See Y. M. Toledano, *Ozar Genazim* (Jerusalem, 1960), 151.

24. Ludwig Frankl, *Yerushalaymah* (Vienna, 1859), 83. For more on the economic life of the Jews of Rhodes, see my book *The Jews of Rhodes*, chap. 4.

25. Avigdor Levy, "Millet Politics" in *Jews of the Ottoman Empire*, 427.

26. Ibid., 427–28.

Chapter Six: Midrashic/Kabbalistic Judaism

1. A. Ubicini, *Lettres sur la Turquie* (Paris, 1854), 2:377–78. See Lewis, *The Jews of Islam*, 140–41, and 164–65.

2. Charles MacFarlane, *Constantinople in 1828* (London, 1829), 115–26.

3. Julia Pardoe, *The City of the Sultan; and Domestic Manners of the Turks in 1836* (London, 1837), 2:361–63.

4. *Kol Sifrei Rav Yosef Yaavets*, 2:149.

5. *Responsa* (New York, 5727), vol. 4. no. 232.

6. Moshe Hagiz, *Mishnat Hakhamim* (Brooklyn, 5719), nos. 589 and 626.

7. Ibid., nos. 104, 105, 106, 111, 114, 495.

8. Rabbi Eliezer Papo, *Yaalzu Hasidim* (Benei Berak, 5730), 67b.

9. Ibid., in an essay *Maamar ha-Kavod* published at the end of the volume, 115b.

10. *Hemdat ha-Yamim*, volume on Shabbat (Jerusalem, 5763), 28.

11. Ibid., 34.

12. M. H. Luzzatto, *Mesillat Yesharim*, translated by Shraga Silverstein (Jerusalem and New York: Feldheim Publishers, 1987), 17, 21.

13. For more about the *Me'am Lo'ez*, see my book *Voices in Exile*, 103–4. It is commonly believed that Rabbi Huli chose the name of this work based on words in Psalm 114, mentioning a people "of a strange tongue." The word *lo'ez* (*la'az*) refers to a vernacular language, not Hebrew, so that Rabbi Huli's choice of this phrase was meant to convey that his book was written in the vernacular (Ladino). While this is the likely reason for his choice of this title, I suggest that he had another reason for choosing a title from the words of Psalm 114. Verse 7 actually includes words that allude to the author's name: *milifnei adon* huli *aretz, milifnei eloha* yaacov.

14. The translations of this section are those of Paula Ovadia de Benardete, published in a tract, *In Search of Our Sephardic Roots* (New York: Foundation for the Advancement of Sephardic Studies and Culture, 1970), 24ff. Rabbi Aryeh Kaplan translated the *Me'am Lo'ez* into English,

and his translation of the section on the soul is found in his *The Torah Anthology: Me'Am Lo'ez* (New York: Maznaim Publishing Corporation, 1977), 1:236–37.

15. Eliezer Papo, *Pele Yoetz*, section on *ger*.

16. Ibid., section on *tsar*.

17. *Mishnat Hakhamim*, nos. 124, 125, 126.

18. Ibid., no. 713.

19. Paula Ovadia de Benardete, *In Search of Our Sephardic Roots*, 34.

20. *Me'am Lo'ez* on B'reishit 15:11.

21. *Pele Yoetz*, section on *ahavat ish ve-ishah*.

22. Ibid., section on *ashirut* and *aniyut*.

23. *Hemdat ha-Yamim*, volume on the Days of Awe, 117.

24. Michael Yaacov Israel, *Shenoth Yamin* (Izmir, 5620/1860), 1:130b. For more on the blood libel in Rhodes, see my book *The Jews of Rhodes*, 37–39.

Chapter Seven: The Religious/ Social Structure of Life

1. Cited by Benardete, *Hispanic Culture*, 130. See also Michael Molho, *Literatura Sefardita de Oriente* (Madrid: Instituto Arias Montano, 1960), 245–46; and M. D. Gaon's monograph, "*Mishkhiyut Levav al Me'am Lo'ez*," Jerusalem, 1933.

2. Biblical references refer to the commentaries of the *Me'am Lo'ez* on those verses. See also my discussion of the *Me'am Lo'ez* in my book, *Voices in Exile*, 103–4.

3. Louis Landau, "*Itsuvah shel ha-Aggada ha-Darshanit be-Sefer Me'am Lo'ez*," in *The Sephardi and Oriental Jewish Heritage*, ed. I. Ben-Ami, (Jerusalem: Magnes Press, 1982), 213–14, points out that Rabbi Huli tended to rephrase traditional sources so as to conform to the ideas he wished to convey to his readers.

4. Avigdor Levy's introduction to *Jews of the Ottoman Empire*, 92.

5. Esther Benbassa and Aron Rodrigue, *Sephardi Jewry: A History of the Judeo-Spanish Community, 14th–20th Centuries* (Berkeley: University of California Press, 2000), 63.

6. Abraham Almeleh, *Ha-Rishonim le-Zion* (Jerusalem, 5730/ 1970).

7. Meir Benayahu, *Marbitz Torah* (Jerusalem, 1953).

8. Cited by Meir Benayahu, *Rabbi Hayyim Yosef David Azulai* (Jerusalem, 1959), 165.

9. On the virtue of looking down as a sign of humility, see Moshe Hagiz, *Mishnat Hakhamim*, 22b.

10. Benardete, *Hispanic Culture*, 137. A variant of this song is provided by Aron Rodrigue, *French Jews, Turkish Jews* (Bloomington: Indiana University Press, 1990), 35.

11. Cited by Aron Rodrigue, *Jews and Muslims: Images of Sephardi and Eastern Jewries in Modern Times* (Seattle: University of Washington Press, 2003), 117.

12. Weiker, *Ottomans, Turks, and the Jewish Polity*, 218.

13. Benbassa and Rodrigue, *Sephardi Jewry*, 32–33.

14. Israel Moshe Hazan, *Kerah shel Romi* (Livorno, 1876). See Edwin Seroussi, "Rabbi Israel Moshe Hazan on Music," in *Haham Gaon Memorial Volume*, ed. M. D. Angel (New York: Sepher Hermon Press and Sephardic House, 1997), 183–95.

15. See Pamela J. Dorn Sezgin, "Hakhamim, Dervishes, and Court Singers: The Relationship of Ottoman Jewish Music to Classical Turkish Music," in *Jews of the Ottoman Empire*, ed. Levy, 585–632. Among Turkish Jews, *piyyutim* were also known as *pizmonim* or *maftirim*. See also Weiker, *Ottomans, Turks and the Jewish Polity*, 218–19.

16. Lionel Trilling, "Manners, Morals and the Novel," in *The Liberal Imagination* (New York, 1953), 200.

17. Shemtob Gaguine, *Keter Shem Tob*, vol. 1 (London, 1934), 93, relates this custom to the female demon, Lilith. He asserts that the origin of the custom derives from the *Zohar*.

18. See my book *The Jews of Rhodes*, 117–19.

19. Bernard Rottiers, *Monumens de Rhodes* (Brussels, 1828), 347–48.

20. Benardete, *Hispanic Culture*, 133.

21. *Hemdat ha-Yamim*, volume on the High Holy Days, 145–46.

22. The travel account is found in J. D. Eisenstein, *Ozar ha-Masaot* (Tel Aviv, 1969), 241.

23. Rabbi Eliyahu ha-Cohen, *Midrash Talpiot* (Jerusalem, 5757/1997), 1:253–54.

24. See, for example, Gilda Angel, *Sephardic Holiday Cooking* (Mt. Vernon: Decalogue Books, 1986; reprint, 2004).

25. For more detailed discussions of the religious customs of Sephardim, see my book, *The Jews of Rhodes*, chap. 10; Michael Molho, *Usos y Costumbres de los Sefardies de Salonica* (Madrid: Instituto Arias Montano, 1950); and Herbert C. Dobrinsky, *A Treasury of Sephardic Laws and Customs* (Hoboken, NJ: Ktav Publishing House, 1986).

Chapter Eight: Ladino Folklore

1. Benardete, *Hispanic Culture*, 63.

2. See, for example, Luria, *A Study of the Monastir Dialect of Judeo-Spanish*; and my book, *The Jews of Rhodes*, 135.

3. David Romey, "A Study of Spanish Tradition in Isolation as Found in the Romances, Refranes and Storied Folklore of the Seattle Sephardic Community" (M.A. dissertation, University of Washington, Seattle, 1950), 17.

4. Moshe Attias, *Romancero Sephardi* (Jerusalem: Ben Zvi Institute, 1961), 59–153, includes the texts of fifty-seven Ladino songs that can be traced back to medieval Spain.

5. Romey, "A Study of Spanish Tradition," 18.

6. I was raised in the Sephardic community of Seattle, Washington, and well remember our many family gatherings where *romances* were sung. Jews of great piety sang right along with those of lesser piety. I do not remember anyone ever objecting to the singing of love songs by men and women. In the early 1980s, Haham Dr. Solomon Gaon, himself a Judeo-Spanish-speaking rabbi, taught classes in Sephardic folklore at my Congregation Shearith Israel in New York City. I well remember him singing love songs, enthusiastically and nostalgically. Both of us participated in a program of Sephardic culture sponsored by the Hebrew College of Boston. A female soloist sang a selection of *romances*, after which Haham Gaon not only applauded loudly but rose to speak in praise of the singer for her beautiful rendition of the songs. Haham Gaon, who served as chief rabbi of the Spanish and Portuguese Congregations of England and as head of the Sephardic Studies Program of Yeshiva University in New York, was a very prominent Orthodox Sephardic rabbi and a man of impeccable piety.

7. The text and music are in Alberto Hemsi, *Coplas Sefardies*, Op. 8 (Rhodes, 1932), 8 in the section of texts, and beginning on p. 5 in the section of musical notations.

8. Max Grunwald, *Tales, Songs and Folkways of Sephardic Jews* [in Hebrew], ed. Dov Noy (Jerusalem: Magnes Press, 1982), 117ff.

9. Samuel Armistead and Joseph Silverman, *Diez romances hispanicos en un manuscrito sefardi de la isla de Rodas* (Pisa, 1962), 50.

10. Collected by David Romey; see his dissertation, 82.

11. Ibid., 74.

12. Moshe Attias, *Cancionero Yehudi-Sefardi* (Jerusalem: Ben Zvi Institute, 1972), 112–113.

13. Ibid., 186.

14. Ibid., 73.

15. Hemsi, *Coplas Sefardies*, Op. 8, p. 7.

16. Attias, *Cancionero Yehudi-Sefardi*, 97–98.

17. Ibid.,128–29.

18. Grunwald, *Tales, Songs and Folkways of Sephardic Jews.* Summaries of the songs he collected are on p. xxxix–xliv. The texts of nineteen of the songs, and some commentary on them by Batya Maoz, are on pp. 117–81.

19. Aside from references already cited, many other scholars have published books and articles containing collections of *romances.* See the bibliography of Samuel Armistead and Joseph Silverman, eds., *Judeo-Spanish Ballads from New York, Collected by M. J. Benardete* (Berkeley: University of California Press, 1981), 122–38. See also Rina Benmayor, *Romances Judeo-Espanoles de Oriente* (Madrid: Editorial Gredos, 1979).

20. The proverbs quoted in the text are drawn from various sources. I have generally retained the spelling of the original collectors. I have not included accent marks, since Ladino was not originally transcribed with such marks. See Abraham Galante's collection in *Revue Hispanique* (1902): 440–54; Abraham Galante, *Proverbes Judeo-Espagnols* (Istanbul, 1954); Isaac Jack Levy, *Refranero Sefardi* (New York, 1969); Klara Perahya, Suzi de Toledo, Suzi Danon, and Fani Ender, *Erensya Sefaradi (Proverbos i Dicas)* (Istanbul: Gozlem, 1994); and David Romey, "The Ubiquitous Sephardic Proverb," in *Studies in Sephardic Culture,* ed. M. D. Angel (New York: Sepher-Hermon Press and Sephardic House, 1980), 57–64.

21. A number of Sephardic stories, and a discussion about them, can be found in Grunwald, *Tales, Songs and Folkways of Sepharadic Jews,* 20–111. See also the collections by Matilda Koen-Sarano, *Djoha, Ke Dize?* (Jerusalem: Kana, 1991); *Konsejas I Konsejikas del Mundo Djudeo-Espanyol* (Jerusalem: Kana, 1994); *Kuentos del Folklor de la Famiya Djudeo-Espanyola* (Jerusalem: Kana, 1986).

22. H. Shaltiel published the stories of Joha in Ladino, *La Vida de Nasredin Hodja* (Istanbul, 1923).

23. See my book, *The Jews of Rhodes,* 132–34. See also, Marie-Christine Varol, "Recipes of Magic-Religious Medicine as Expressed Linguistically," in *Jews, Turks, Ottomans,* ed. Avigdor Levy (Syracuse, NY: Syracuse University Press, 2002), 260–71; Melvin Firestone, "Sephardic Folk-Curing in Seattle," *Journal of American Folklore* 75 (1962): 301–10; Weiker, *Ottomans, Turks and the Jewish Polity,* 221; and my article, "Seguloth in a Manuscript from the Island of Rhodes," *Estudios Sefardies,* Instituto Arias Montano, Madrid, no. 1 (1978): 83–89.

24. Benardete, *Hispanic Culture,* 142–43. The English translation of Levy's text is Benardete's.

Chapter Nine: Confronting Modernity

1. See Avigdor Levy's introduction to *Jews of the Ottoman Empire*, 98f.

2. Cited in the introduction of Braude and Lewis to *Christians and Jews in the Ottoman Empire*, 1: 30.

3. Hasan Kayali, "Jewish Representation in the Ottoman Parliaments," in *The Jews of the Ottoman Empire*, ed. Levy, 508–509.

4. Avigdor Levy, introduction to *Jews of the Ottoman Empire*, 101–2.

5. Ibid., 105–6.

6. Cited by Aron Rodrigue, "The Beginnings of Westernization and Reform," in *The Jews of the Ottoman Empire*, ed. Levy, 441.

7. Ibid., 442–43.

8. Ibid., 448–49; Benardete, *Hispanic Culture*, 144–46.

9. See Rodrigue, *French Jews, Turkish Jews*, 37; and Shalom Goldman, *God's Sacred Tongue* (Chapel Hill: University of North Carolina Press, 2004), 148.

10. Avigdor Levy's introduction to *Jews of the Ottoman Empire*, 110.

11. Ibid., 110–11.

12. Published in Bucharest, 5620/1860.

13. Rabbi Bibas is quoted in Andrew Bonar, *Narrative of A Mission of Inquiry to the Jews from the Church of Scotland in 1839* (Philadelphia, 1839), 395. See also pp. 380, 392–93, 396, 526.

14. Yehudah Alkalai, *Kol Korei*, in *Kitvei ha-Rav Yehudah Alkalai*, ed. Isaac Rafael (Jerusalem: Mosad haRav Kook, 1974), 1:280–82, 287.

15. Ibid., *Goral Hashem*, 542–43.

16. This appeal was printed by the Alliance in 1860. The English translation cited in the text is from Aron Rodrigue, *Jews and Muslims: Images of Sephardi and Eastern Jewries in Modern Times*, 8–9.

17. For more on the role of the Alliance schools, see Rodrigue, ibid.; and also his *French Jews, Turkish Jews*; and his and Esther Benbassa's book, *Sephardi Jewry*, 83ff. See also Paul Dumont, "Jewish Communities in Turkey during the Last Decades of the Nineteenth Century in the Light of the Archives of the Alliance Israélite Universelle," in *Christians and Jews in the Ottoman Empire*, ed. Braude and Lewis, 1:209–42.

18. See my book *Voices in Exile*, chap. 10; and David Benveniste, *"Ribi Yehudah Yaacov Nehama: Mevaser Tekufat ha-Haskalah be-Saloniki,"* in *The Sephardi and Oriental Jewish Heritage*, ed. Issachar Ben-Ami, 25–34; and Joseph Papo, "Nissim Behar: A Sephardi Innovator," *Midstream* 38:3 (March 1987): 44–46.

19. "Associational Strategies," in *The Jews of the Ottoman Empire*, ed. A. Levy, 457–84.

20. Avner Levy, "*Alexander Benguiat uTmurato le-Itonut veha-Sifrut ha-Yafa be-Ladino.*" in *The Sephardi and Oriental Jewish Heritage,* ed. Ben-Ami, 205–12. See also my article, "Elia Carmona: Judeo-Spanish Author," in *Jewish Book Annual* 44 (1986/87): 132–40; and Benbassa and Rodrigue, *Sephardi Jewry,* 110ff. For a study of the first Ladino newspaper in the United States, see my book *La America: The Sephardic Experience in the United States* (Philadelphia: Jewish Publication Society, 1982).

21. Benbassa and Rodrigue, *Sephardi Jewry,* 268–70.

22. Cited by Avigdor Levy in his introduction to *Jews of the Ottoman Empire,* 123.

23. "The Balkan Wars and the Jews," *American Jewish Yearbook* 15 (1913–14): 186–206. See especially 189–95.

24. Aron Rodrigue, "Eastern Sephardi Jewry and the Balkans," in *Sephardi and Middle Eastern Jewries,* ed. Goldberg, 84–85.

25. Hayyim J. Cohen, *The Jews of the Middle East, 1860–1972* (New Brunswick: Transaction Books, 1973), 76ff.

26. See my book *La America: The Sephardic Experience in the United States,* for a study of the American experience of Jews of Judeo-Spanish background.

27. See Tracy Harris, *Death of a Language: The History of Judeo-Spanish* (Newark: University of Delaware Press, 1994). See also Karen Gerson's master's dissertation, "Language Change as Influenced by Cultural Contact: A Case: Ladino" (Bogazici University, 1983); and especially Haim Vidal Sephiha, *L'Agonie des Judeo-Espagnols* (Paris: Editions Entente, 1977).

Chapter Ten: Lasting Lessons

1. H. Y. D. Azulai, *Avodat ha-Kodesh* (Warsaw, 5639/1879), 6.

2. Rabbi Eliezer Papo, *Pele Yoetz,* section on *hitbod'dut.*

3. Rabbi Elazar Azikri, *Sefer Hareidim* (Jerusalem, 5744/ 1983), 71.

4. Daniel J. Elazar, "Sephardim and Ashkenazim: The Classic and Romantic Traditions in Jewish Civilization," *Judaism* 33 (1984): 154.

5. Abraham Joshua Heschel, *The Earth Is the Lord's* (New York: Henry Schuman, 1950), 34–35.

6. Andre Chouraqui, *Between East and West* (Philadelphia: Jewish Publication Society, 1968), 63.

7. Michael Molho, *Usos y costumbres de los Sefardies de Salonica,* 155.

8. Elazar's article in *Judaism* 33 (Spring 1984): 156. See also his article, "Can Sephardic Judaism Be Reconstructed?" *Judaism* 41 (Summer 1992): 220–21.

9. Rabbi Reuben Eliyahu Israel, *Pirkei Avot* (Izmir, 1924). See my article, "The *Pirkei Avot* of Reuben Eliyahu Israel," *Tradition* 11 (Spring 1971): 92–98.

10. Raphael Patai, "Sephardi World View and the Haskala," *The Alliance Review* (Fall 1975): 16–17.

11. Nahum Glatzer, *Franz Rosenzweig: His Life and Thought* (Philadelphia: Jewish Publication Society, 1953), 51. See also Yosef Hayim Yerushalmi, "In Praise of Ladino," *Conservative Judaism* 27 (Winter 1973): 57.

12. Jose Faur, *Rabbi Yisrael Moshe Hazzan: The Man and His Works* (Haifa: Raphael Arbel Academic Publishers, 1978), 6. See also Faur's article, "Sephardim in the Nineteenth Century: New Directions and Old Values," *Proceedings of the American Academy for Jewish Research* 44 (1977): 29–52.

Selected Bibliography

Almeleh, Abraham. *Ha-Rishonim le-Zion.* Jerusalem: Rubin Mass, 5730/1970.

Angel, Gilda. *Sephardic Holiday Cooking: Recipes and Traditions.* Mt. Vernon, NY: Decalogue Books, 1986. Reprint 2004.

Angel, Marc D. "Elia Carmona: Judeo-Spanish Author." *Jewish Book Annual* 44 (1986): 132–40.

———. "Folk Wisdom and Intellectual Wisdom: A Study in Sephardic Culture." In *Hommage A Haim Vidal Sephiha,* edited by Winfried Busse and Marie-Christine Varol-Bornes, 391–97. Berne: Peter Lang, 1996.

———. *The Jews of Rhodes: The History of a Sephardic Community.* New York: Sepher-Hermon Press, 1978. Reprints 1980 and 1998.

———. *La America: The Sephardic Experience in the United States.* Philadelphia: Jewish Publication Society, 1982.

———. *Loving Truth and Peace: The Grand Religious Worldview of Rabbi Benzion Uziel.* Northvale, NJ: Jason Aronson, 1999.

———. *The Rhythms of Jewish Living: A Sephardic Approach.* New York: Sepher-Hermon Press, 1986. Reprint 1997.

———. "The Sephardic Communities of the Eastern Mediterranean Islands." In *The Sephardi Heritage,* edited by R. Barnett and W. Schwab, 2: 115–430. Grendon, England: Gibraltar Books, 1989.

———. *Voices in Exile: A Study in Sephardic Intellectual History.* Hoboken, N.J.: Ktav Publishing House, 1991.

Armistead, Samuel, and Joseph Silverman. *Diez romances hispanicos en un manuscrito de la isla de Rodas.* Pisa, 1962.

___, eds. *Judeo-Spanish Ballads from New York, Collected by M. J. Benardete.* Berkeley: University of California Press, 1981.

Attias, Moshe. *Cancionero Yehudi-Sefardi.* Jerusalem: Ben Zvi Institute, 1972.

———. *Romancero Sephardi.* Jerusalem: Ben Zvi Institute, 1961.

Barnai, Jacob. "*Ha-Yehudim be-Empiriah ha-Ottomanit.*" In *History of the Jews in Islamic Countries,* edited by Shemuel Ettinger, 1:73–118, 2:183–297, 3:89–183. Jerusalem: Merkaz Zalman Shazar, 1981–86.

Baron, Salo W. *A Social and Religious History of the Jews,* vol. 18. New York: Columbia University Press, 1983.

Ben-Ami, Issachar, ed. *The Sephardi and Oriental Jewish Heritage.* Jerusalem: Magnes Press, 1982.

Benardete, Mair Jose. *Hispanic Culture and Character of the Sephardic Jews.* New York: Hispanic Institute, 1952. Reprint New York: Sepher-Hermon Press and Sephardic House, 1982.

Benayahu, Meir. *Marbitz Torah.* Jerusalem, 1953.

———. *Rabbi Hayyim Yosef David Azulai.* Jerusalem, 1959.

Benbassa, Esther, and Aron Rodrigue. *Sephardi Jewry: A History of the Judeo-Spanish Community, 14th–20th Centuries.* Berkeley: University of California Press, 2000.

Benmayor, Rina. *Romances Judeo-Espanoles de Oriente.* Madrid: Editorial Gredos, 1979.

Ben-Sasson, Hayyim Hillel. "*Galut u-Geulah be-Einav shel Dor Golei Sefarad.*" In *Sefer ha-Yovel le-Yitshak Baer,* edited by Sh. Ettinger et al., 23–64. Jerusalem, 5721/1961.

———. "*Kinah al Gerush Sefarad.*" *Tarbitz* 3 (1961): 59–71.

Bentov, Hayyim. "*Shitat Limud ha-Talmud b'Yeshivot Saloniki ve-Turkia.*" *Sefunot* 13 (5731/1971): 5–102.

Bornes-Varol, Marie-Christine. "The Balat Quarter and Its Image." In *The Jews of the Ottoman Empire,* edited by Avigdor Levy, 633–44. Princeton, NJ: Darwin Press, 1994.

Braude, Benjamin, and Bernard Lewis, eds. *Christians and Jews in the Ottoman Empire,* 2 vols. New York and London: Holmes and Meier, 1982.

Braudel, Fernand. *The Mediterranean,* 2 vols. New York: Harper and Row, 1966, 1973.

Carlebach, Elisheva. *The Pursuit of Heresy: Rabbi Moses Hagiz and the Sabbatian Controversies.* New York: Columbia University Press, 1990.

Chouraqui, Andre. *Between East and West: A History of the Jews of North Africa.* Philadelphia: Jewish Publication Society, 1968.

Cohen, Amnon. *Jewish Life Under Islam: Jerusalem in the Sixteenth Century.* Cambridge, MA: Harvard University Press, 1984.

Cohen, Hayyim J. *The Jews of the Middle East, 1860–1972.* New Brunswick, NJ: Transaction Books, 1973.

Dan, Joseph. *Jewish Mysticism and Jewish Ethics.* Seattle: University of Washington Press, 1986.

Dobrinsky, Herbert C. *A Treasury of Sephardic Laws and Customs*. Hoboken, NJ: Ktav Publishing House, 1986.

Elazar, Daniel, ed. *The Balkan Jewish Communities*. Lanham, MD: University Press of America, 1984.

———. "Can Sephardic Judaism be Reconstructed?" *Judaism* 41 (1992): 217–28.

———. "Sephardim and Ashkenazim: The Classic and Romantic Traditions in Jewish Civilization." *Judaism* 33 (1984): 146–59.

Epstein, Mark. "The Leadership of the Ottoman Jews in the Fifteenth and Sixteenth Centuries." In *Christians and Jews in the Ottoman Empire*, edited by B. Braude and B. Lewis, 1:101–15. New York and London: Holmes and Meier, 1982.

———. *The Ottoman Jewish Communities and Their Role in the Fifteenth and Sixteenth Centuries*. Freiburg, Germany: Klaus Schwarz Verlag, 1980.

Faur, Jose. *Rabbi Yisrael Moshe Hazzan: The Man and His Works*. Haifa: Raphael Arbel Academic Publishers, 1978.

———. "Sephardim in the Nineteenth Century: New Directions and Old Values." *Proceedings of the American Academy for Jewish Research* 44 (1977): 29–52.

Firestone, Melvin. "Sephardic Folk-Curing in Seattle." *Journal of American Folklore* 75 (1962): 301–310.

Galante, Abraham. "Judeo-Spanish Proverbs." *Revue Hispanique* (1902): 440–54.

———. *Proverbes Judeo-Espagnols*. Istanbul, 1954.

Gaon, M. D. *Mishkhiyut Levav al Me'am Lo'ez*. Jerusalem, 1933.

Gerber, Hayyim. *The Jews of the Ottoman Empire in the Sixteenth and Seventeenth Centuries* [in Hebrew]. Jerusalem: Historical Society of Israel, 1982.

Gerson, Karen. "Language Change as Influenced by Cultural Contact: A Case: Ladino." Master's dissertation, Bogazici University, 1983.

Goitein, S. D. *Jews and Arabs*. New York: Schocken Books, 1974.

Goldberg, Harvey E., ed. *Sephardi and Middle Eastern Jewries: History and Culture in the Modern Era*. Bloomington: Indiana University Press, 1996.

Goldish, Matt. *The Sabbatean Prophets*. Cambridge, MA: Harvard University Press, 2004.

Grunwald, Max. *Tales, Songs and Folkways of Sephardic Jews* [in Hebrew], edited by Dov Noy. Jerusalem: Magnes Press, 1982.

Hacker, Joseph. "The Intellectual Activity of the Jews of the Ottoman Empire During the Sixteenth and Seventeenth Centuries." In *Jewish Thought in the Seventeenth Century*, edited by I. Twersky and B. Septimus, 95–135. Cambridge: Harvard University Press, 1987.

————. "Jewish Autonomy in the Ottoman Empire." In *The Jews of the Ottoman Empire*, edited by A. Levy, 153–202. Princeton, NJ: Darwin Press, 1994.

————. *"Lidmutam ha-Ruhanit shel Yehudei Sefarad be-Sof ha-Meah he-Hamesh Esrei." Sefunot* 17 (5743/1983): 21–95.

————. "Ottoman Policy toward the Jews and Jewish Attitudes toward the Ottomans during the Fifteenth Century." In *Christians and Jews in the Ottoman Empire*, edited by B. Braude and B. Lewis, 117–126. New York and London: Holmes and Meier, 1982.

Hacker, Louis. "The Communal Life of the Sephardic Jews in New York City." *Jewish Social Service Quarterly* 3 (1926): 32–40.

Harris, Tracy. *Death of a Language: The History of Judeo-Spanish.* Newark: University of Delaware Press, 1994.

Hemsi, Alberto. *Coplas Sefardies.* Alexandria, Egypt, 1932–37.

Kalderon, Albert. *Abraham Galante: A Biography.* New York: Sepher-Hermon Press and Sephardic House, 1983.

Koen-Sarano, Matilda. *Djoha, Ke Dize.* Jerusalem: Kana, 1991.

————. *Konsejas I Konsejikas del Mundo Djudeo-Espanyol.* Jerusalem: Kana, 1994.

————. *Kuentos del Folklor de la Famiya Djudeo-Espanyola.* Jerusalem: Kana, 1986.

Landau, Jacob. *Jews in Nineteenth Century Egypt.* New York: New York University Press, 1969.

Levy, Avigdor, ed. *Jews, Turks, Ottomans: A Shared History, Fifteenth Through the Twentieth Centuries.* Syracuse, NY: Syracuse University Press, 2002.

————, ed. *The Jews of the Ottoman Empire.* Princeton, NY: Darwin Press, 1994.

Levy, Isaac J. *Refranero Sefardi.* New York, 1969.

Levy, Reuben. *The Social Structure of Islam.* Cambridge: Cambridge University Press, 1971.

Lewis, Bernard. *The Emergence of Modern Turkey.* London: Oxford University Press, 1961.

————. *The Jews of Islam.* Princeton, NJ: Princeton University Press, 1984.

Luria, Max. *A Study of the Monastir Dialect of Judeo-Spanish.* New York and Paris: Revue Hispanique, 1930.

Molho, Michael. *Literatura Sefardita de Oriente.* Madrid: Instituto Arias Montano, 1960.

————. *Usos y Costumbres de los Sefardies de Salonica.* Madrid: Instituto Arias Montano, 1950.

Nehama, Joseph. *Histoire des Israelites de Salonique.* Paris, 1935.

Patai, Raphael. "Sephardi World View and the Haskala." *The Alliance Review* (Fall 1975): 16–20.

Perahya, Suzi de Toledo, Suzi Danon, and Fani Ender, eds. *Erensya Sefaradi (Proverbos I Dicas)*. Istanbul: Gozlem, 1994.

Pool, David de Sola. "The Immigration of Levantine Jews into the United States." *Jewish Charities* (April 1914): 12–27.

———. "The Levantine Jews in the United States." *American Jewish Yearbook* 15 (1913/14): 207–20.

Rodrigue, Aron. *French Jews, Turkish Jews*. Bloomington: Indiana University Press, 1990.

———. *Jews and Muslims: Images of Sephardi and Eastern Jewries in Modern Times*. Seattle: University of Washington Press, 2003.

Romey, David. "A Study of Spanish Tradition in Isolation as Found in the Romances, Refranes and Storied Folklore of the Seattle Sephardic Community." M.A. dissertation, University of Washington, Seattle, 1950.

———. "The Ubiquitous Sephardic Proverb." In *Studies in Sephardic Culture*, edited by M. D. Angel, 57–64. New York: Sepher-Hermon Press and Sephardic House, 1980.

Rosanes, Solomon. *Dibrei Yemei Yisrael be-Togarmah* and *Korot ha-Yehudim be-Turkiah ve-Artsot ha-Kedem*, 6 vols. 1907–45.

Roth, Cecil. *The House of Nasi: Dona Gracia*. Philadelphia: Jewish Publication Society, 1947. Reprinted with introduction by H. P. Salomon. New York: Sepher-Hermon Press, 1974.

———. *The House of Nasi: The Duke of Naxos*. Philadelphia: Jewish Publication Society, 1948.

Salomon, Herman P. "Myth or Anti-Myth? The Oldest Accounts Concerning the Origin of Portuguese Judaism at Amsterdam." In *Two Portuguese Studies*, 105–61. Braga, Portugal, 1991.

Schechter, Solomon. "Safed in the Sixteenth Century." *Studies in Judaism*, 2nd ser. 202–306. Philadelphia: Jewish Publication Society, 1908.

Scholem, Gershom. *Sabbatai Sevi*. Princeton: Princeton University Press, 1973.

Sciaky, Leon. *Farewell to Salonica*. New York: Current Books, 1946.

Sephiha, Haim Vidal. *L'Agonie des Judeo-Espagnols*. Paris: Editions Entente, 1977.

Seroussi, Edwin. "Rabbi Israel Moshe Hazan on Music." In *Haham Gaon Memorial Volume*, edited by M. D. Angel, 183–95. New York: Sepher-Hermon Press and Sephardic House, 1997.

Shaw, Stanford. *The Jews of the Ottoman Empire and the Turkish Republic*. New York: New York University Press, 1991.

Shaw, Stanford, and Ezel Kural Shaw. *History of the Ottoman Empire and Modern Turkey*. Cambridge: Cambridge University Press, 1977.

Stillman, Norman. *The Jews of Arab Lands: A History and Source Book*. Philadephia: Jewish Publication Society, 1975.

————. *The Jews of Arab Lands in Modern Times*. Philadelphia: Jewish Publication Society, 2003.

Tamir, Vicki. *Bulgaria and Her Jews*. New York: Sepher-Hermon Press, 1979.

Weiker, Walter. *Ottomans, Turks and the Jewish Polity: A History of The Jews of Turkey*. Jerusalem: Jerusalem Center for Public Affairs, 1992.

Werblowsky, R. J. Z. *Joseph Karo*. Philadelphia: Jewish Publication Society, 1977.

Yaari, Abraham. *Ha-Defus ha-Ivri be-Kushta*. Jerusalem: Magnes Press, 1967.

Yerushalmi, Yosef Hayim. *From Spanish Court to Italian Ghetto*. New York: Columbia University Press, 1971.

Zimmels, H. J. "The Contributions of the Sephardim to the Responsa Literature Till the Beginning of the Sixteenth Century." In *The Sephardi Heritage*, edited by R. Barnett, 1:367–401. New York: Ktav Publishing House, 1971.

Zohar, Zvi. *The Luminous Face of the East: Studies in the Legal and Religious Thought of Sephardic Rabbis of the Middle East*. Tel Aviv: HaKibbutz HaMeuhad Press, 2001.

Index

About Jewish Lights

People of all faiths and backgrounds yearn for books that attract, engage, educate, and spiritually inspire.

Our principal goal is to stimulate thought and help all people learn about who the Jewish People are, where they come from, and what the future can be made to hold. While people of our diverse Jewish heritage are the primary audience, our books speak to people in the Christian world as well and will broaden their understanding of Judaism and the roots of their own faith.

We bring to you authors who are at the forefront of spiritual thought and experience. While each has something different to say, they all say it in a voice that you can hear.

Our books are designed to welcome you and then to engage, stimulate, and inspire. We judge our success not only by whether or not our books are beautiful and commercially successful, but by whether or not they make a difference in your life.

For your information and convenience, at the back of this book we have provided a list of other Jewish Lights books you might find interesting and useful. They cover all the categories of your life:

Bar/Bat Mitzvah	Life Cycle
Bible Study / Midrash	Meditation
Children's Books	Parenting
Congregation Resources	Prayer
Current Events / History	Ritual / Sacred Practice
Ecology	Spirituality
Fiction: Mystery, Science Fiction	Theology / Philosophy
Grief / Healing	Travel
Holidays / Holy Days	Twelve Steps
Inspiration	Women's Interest
Kabbalah / Mysticism / Enneagram	

Rabbi Marc D. Angel, PhD, is rabbi emeritus of the Spanish and Portuguese Synagogue, Congregation Shearith Israel of New York City (founded 1654). He is the founder and director of the Institute for Jewish Ideas and Ideals (www.jewishideas.org) and co-founder of the International Rabbinic Fellowship, a worldwide association of modern Orthodox rabbis. Raised in a Judeo-Spanish family, Rabbi Angel has been researching and writing about Sephardic culture for over thirty years. He is author of *Voices in Exile: A Study in Sephardic Intellectual History*, the editor of *Exploring Sephardic Customs and Traditions* and many more books and articles.

"Captures the essence of the Sephardic Ottoman world with sensitivity, nuance and love. Exudes warmth and pride as well as much valuable information. No cultural expression of the Sephardic Jew is ignored in this enduring work of great charm and learning."
—**Professor Jane S. Gerber**, director, Center for Jewish Studies and the Institute for Sephardic Studies, Graduate Center of the City University of New York

"A loving, critical, and wistful look at the inner life of the Sephardim. Will be cherished by Sephardim and Ashkenazim alike. Indeed, Ashkenazim will note the intriguing parallels to their own history."
—**Dr. Norman Lamm**, chancellor, Yeshiva University

"A great read and important book illuminating the post inquisition destiny and rich spiritual development of the Judeo-Spanish Sephardic community in the Ottoman Empire—an essential and often neglected integral part of the overall Jewish experience."
—**David E. R. Dangoor**, president, American Sephardi Federation

"This valuable historical journey demonstrates the 'triumph of the human spirit,' resolute in its optimism and dignity."   —***Publishers Weekly***

"Highly readable.... Successfully maneuvers through the sprawling history of Judeo-Spanish civilization while skillfully incorporating a great many lively details."   —***Jewish Book World***

"Provides a thorough survey of culture, history and religious foundations.... An essential study for any who would understand the history of Sephardic belief and evolution."   —***Midwest Book Review***

JEWISH LIGHTS Publishing
www.jewishlights.com

Printed in the USA
CPSIA information can be obtained
at www.ICGtesting.com
JSHW012027140824
68134JS00033B/2924